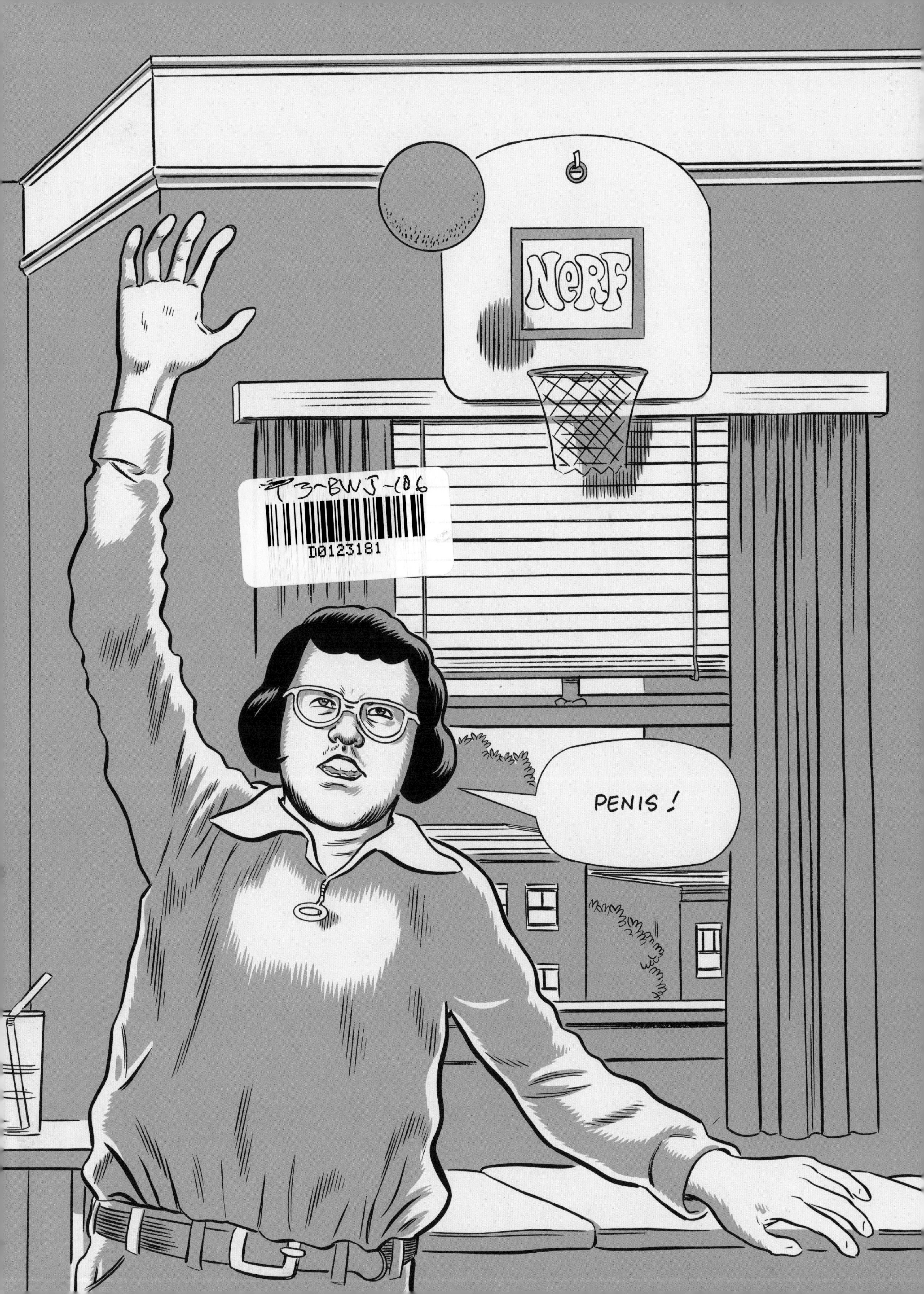
NeRF
PENIS !

THE DEATH-RAY

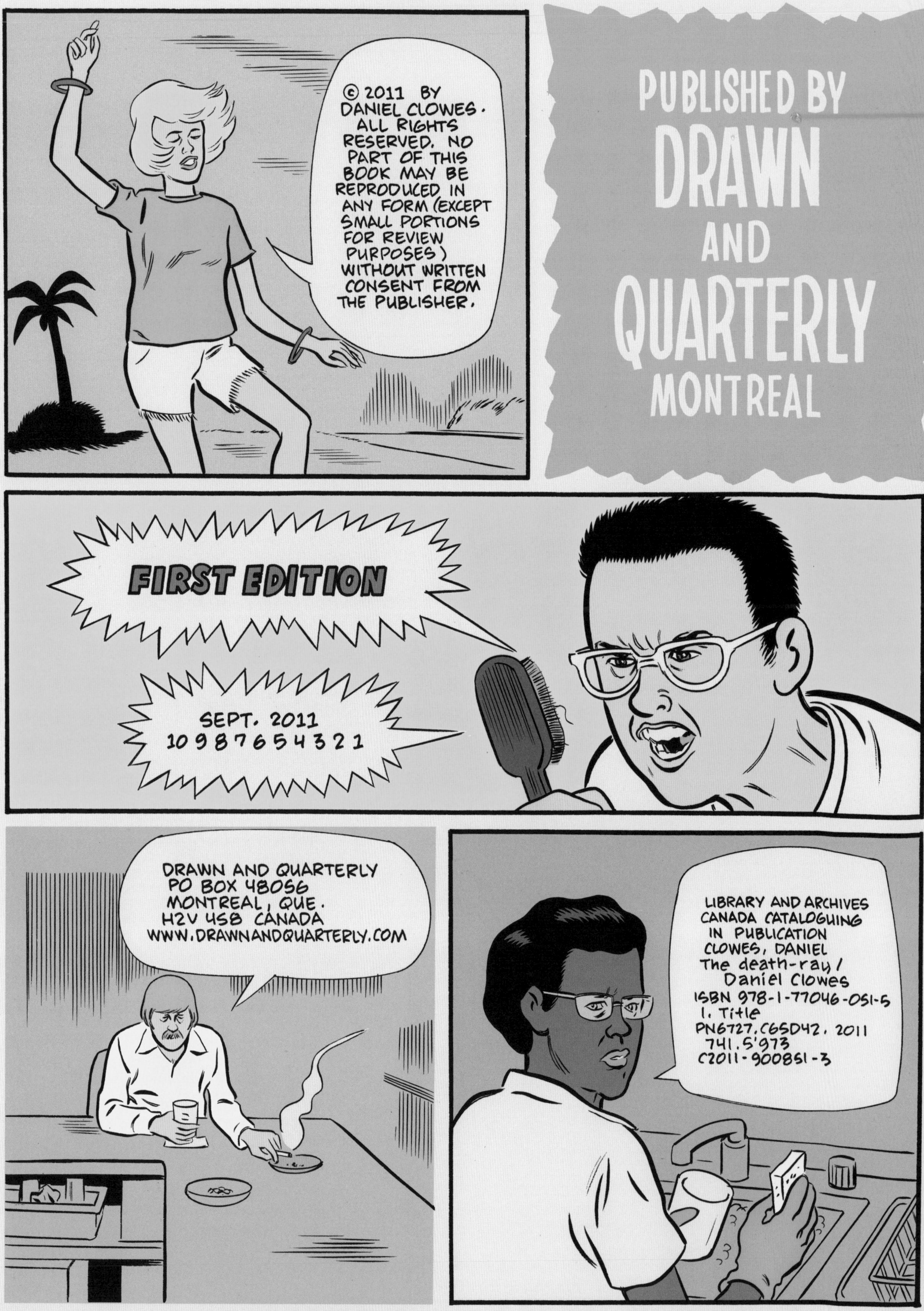
© 2011 BY DANIEL CLOWES. ALL RIGHTS RESERVED. NO PART OF THIS BOOK MAY BE REPRODUCED IN ANY FORM (EXCEPT SMALL PORTIONS FOR REVIEW PURPOSES) WITHOUT WRITTEN CONSENT FROM THE PUBLISHER.
PUBLISHED BY DRAWN AND QUARTERLY MONTREAL
FIRST EDITION
SEPT. 2011
10 9 8 7 6 5 4 3 2 1
DRAWN AND QUARTERLY
PO BOX 48056
MONTREAL, QUE.
H2V 4S8 CANADA
WWW.DRAWNANDQUARTERLY.COM
LIBRARY AND ARCHIVES CANADA CATALOGUING IN PUBLICATION
CLOWES, DANIEL
The death-ray / Daniel Clowes
ISBN 978-1-77046-051-5
1. Title
PN6727.C65D42. 2011
741.5'973
C2011-900851-3

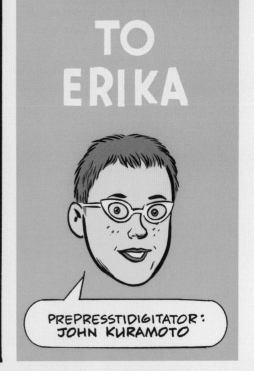

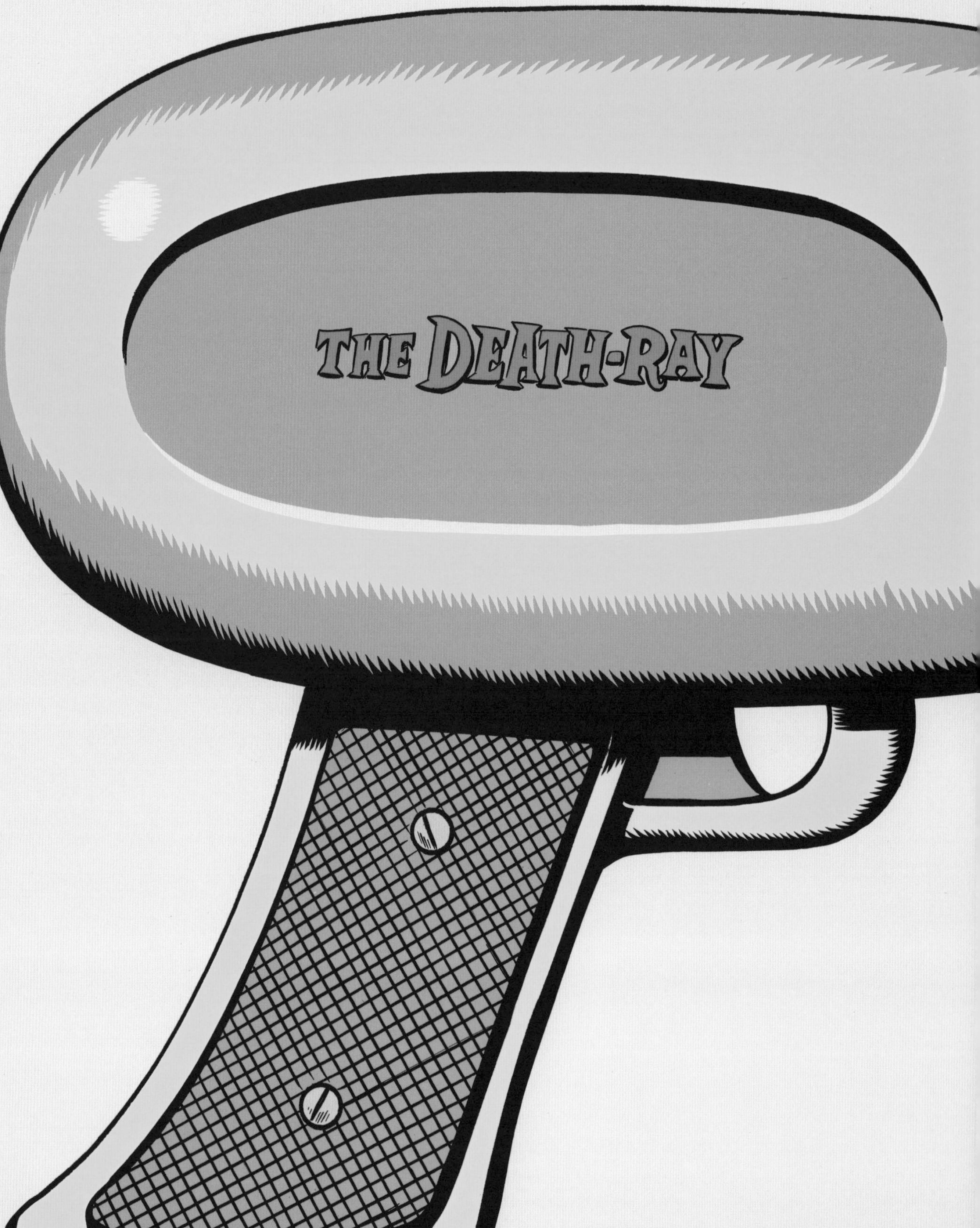
THE DEATH-RAY

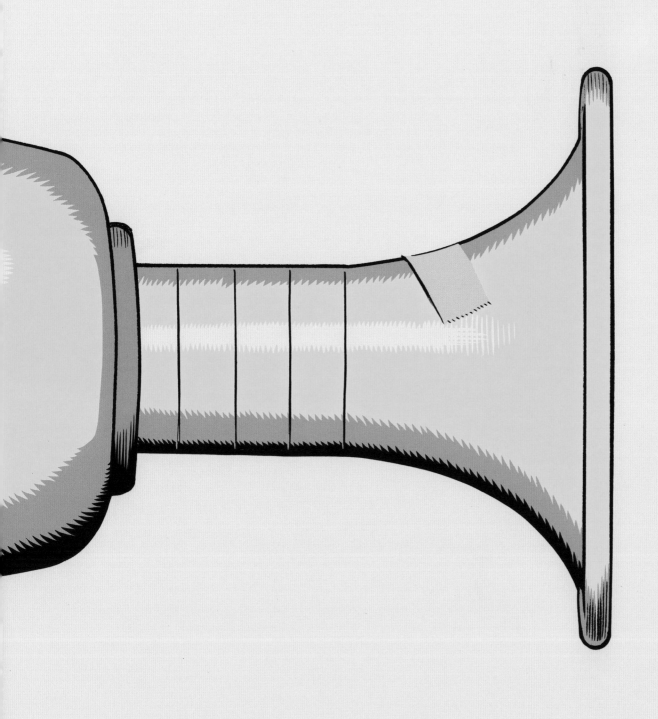

THE ORIGIN OF

MY MOM.

I DIDN'T KNOW YOU HAD A MOM.

HOW COULD I NOT HAVE A MOM?

WHERE IS SHE?

DEAD FROM A BLOOD CLOT IN THE BRAIN.

SO THEN IS PAPPY YOUR DAD?

NOPE-- MY GRANDPA.

WHERE'S YOUR REAL DAD?

DEAD, TOO, DEAD FROM CANCER.

I WISH MY PARENTS WERE DEAD.

THAT'S REALLY STUPID. YOU'RE A TOTALLY IGNORANT IMBECILE.

MY DAD WAS A FAMOUS SCIENTIST. HE USED TO WORK AT A LAB IN TENNESSEE. HE MET MY MOM WHILE SHE WAS WORKING AT A RESTAURANT. SHE WAS ONLY TWENTY-TWO WHEN SHE DIED.

SO THEN MY DAD AND I CAME HERE TO LIVE WITH MY GRANDPARENTS, AND AFTER HE DIED THEY RAISED ME AS THEIR OWN.

WHERE'S PAPPY'S WIFE?

SHE'S DEAD TOO.

2.

ANDY

AND THEN MY GRANDMOTHER DIED, SO NOW IT'S JUST ME AND PAPPY.

SHIT, MAN...

SHH!

HE CAN'T HEAR US.

SOME-TIMES HE CAN...

JUST DON'T SWEAR.

HOW'S YOUR GIRLFRIEND?

FINE.

YOU NEVER FUCKED HER, HUH?

SHH!

HOW DO YOU KNOW SHE'S NOT SCREWING A LOT OF OTHER GUYS OUT IN CALIFORNIA?

ANOTHER PART OF MY STORY IS THAT IN 1973 MY DAD AND I MOVED TO LIVERMORE, CA. FOR A YEAR AND THAT'S WHEN I MET MY GIRLFRIEND DUSTY. SHE LIVED NEXT DOOR AND NOW WE WRITE TO EACH OTHER ALL THE TIME.

SHE'S NOT LIKE THAT.

WHAT'S GONNA HAPPEN TO YOU IF PAPPY EVER DIES?

SHH!

HOW COME YOU'RE SO INTERESTED IN ME ALL OF A SUDDEN?

BECAUSE YOU'RE JUST ABOUT THE ONLY GUY IN SCHOOL I CAN STAND...YOU'RE A GOOD GUY; YOU HAVEN'T HAD IT EASY LIKE THE REST OF THEM...

I DON'T FEEL SORRY FOR MYSELF, BUT SOMETIMES I THINK ALL THESE TRAGEDIES COULDN'T JUST BE A COINCIDENCE. MAYBE IT MEANS SOMETHING. MAYBE I'M DESTINED FOR SOMETHING BIG.

THAT'S FOR SURE.

   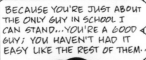  

3.

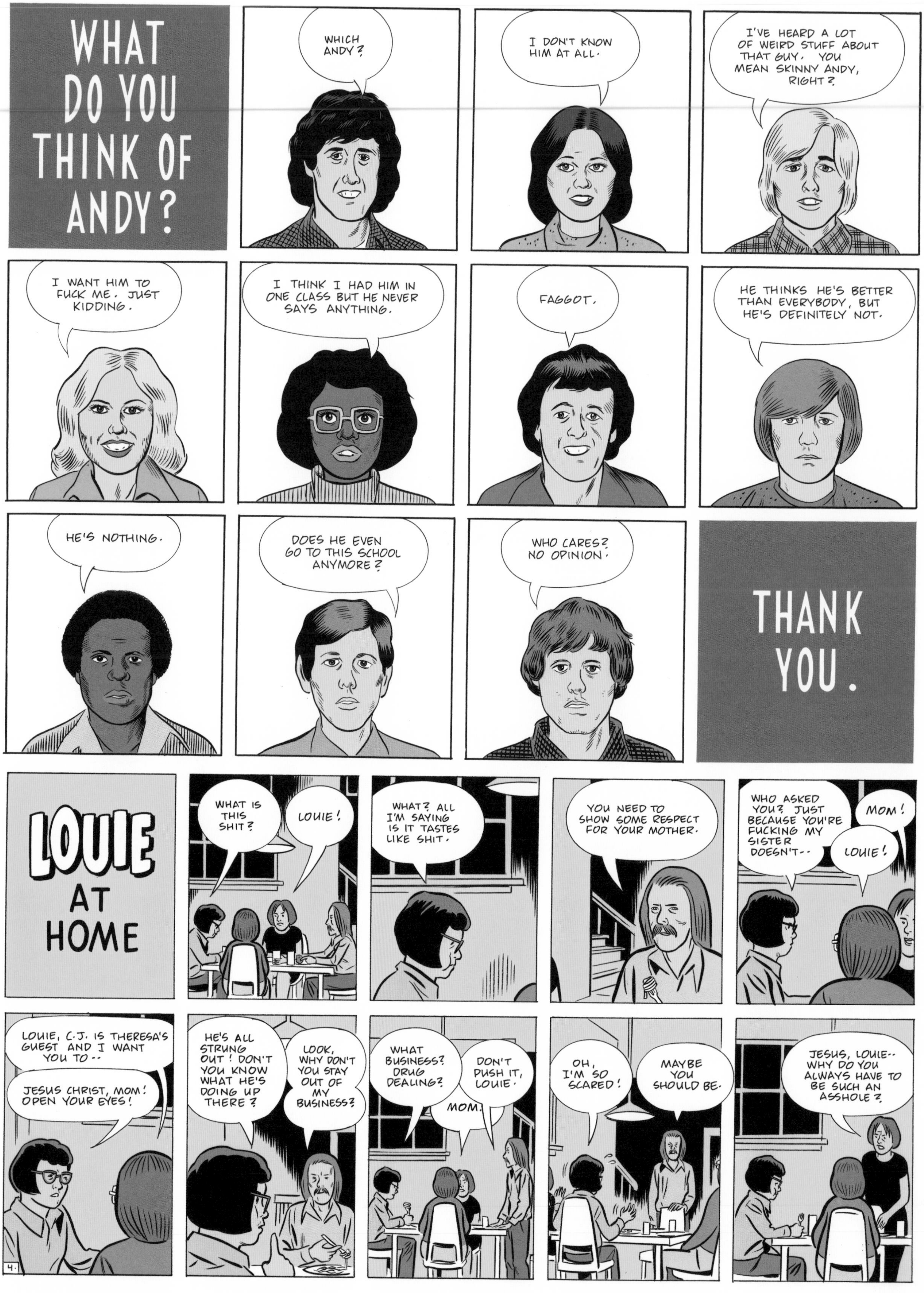
WHAT DO YOU THINK OF ANDY?
WHICH ANDY?
I DON'T KNOW HIM AT ALL.
I'VE HEARD A LOT OF WEIRD STUFF ABOUT THAT GUY. YOU MEAN SKINNY ANDY, RIGHT?
I WANT HIM TO FUCK ME. JUST KIDDING.
I THINK I HAD HIM IN ONE CLASS BUT HE NEVER SAYS ANYTHING.
FAGGOT.
HE THINKS HE'S BETTER THAN EVERYBODY, BUT HE'S DEFINITELY NOT.
HE'S NOTHING.
DOES HE EVEN GO TO THIS SCHOOL ANYMORE?
WHO CARES? NO OPINION.
THANK YOU.
LOUIE AT HOME
WHAT IS THIS SHIT?
LOUIE!
WHAT? ALL I'M SAYING IS IT TASTES LIKE SHIT.
YOU NEED TO SHOW SOME RESPECT FOR YOUR MOTHER.
WHO ASKED YOU? JUST BECAUSE YOU'RE FUCKING MY SISTER DOESN'T--
MOM!
LOUIE!
LOUIE, C.J. IS THERESA'S GUEST AND I WANT YOU TO--
JESUS CHRIST, MOM! OPEN YOUR EYES!
HE'S ALL STRUNG OUT! DON'T YOU KNOW WHAT HE'S DOING UP THERE?
LOOK, WHY DON'T YOU STAY OUT OF MY BUSINESS?
WHAT BUSINESS? DRUG DEALING?
DON'T PUSH IT, LOUIE.
MOM.
OH, I'M SO SCARED!
MAYBE YOU SHOULD BE.
JESUS, LOUIE-- WHY DO YOU ALWAYS HAVE TO BE SUCH AN ASSHOLE?

ANDY'S WORLD

C'MON ANDY!

HUFF!

OKAY, I'LL GIVE YOU 4.
STOOB!

PUFF PUFF

PUFF PUFF
SLOW IT DOWN, STOOB!
PACE YOUR-SELF!

NGGH
OKAY, THAT'S ENOUGH.
27 FOR STOOB!

LOUIE! YOU'RE UP!

PUFF PUFF PUFF PUFF PUFF PUFF PUFF

PUFF PUFF PUFF PUFF
LOOK AT LOUIE!

PUFF PUFF PUFF PUFF PUFF
LOUIE PUT ON SOME MUSCLE OVER THE SUMMER!

PUFF PUFF
28!

LOU-IE!
WAY TO GO, LOUIE!

C'MON, LET'S GO.

LOU-IE!
JUST A SECOND...

HEY...

HEY STOOB, I JUST WANTED TO SAY THAT I GOT REALLY LUCKY OUT THERE TODAY... YOU JUST NEEDED TO PACE YOURSELF A LITTLE BETTER, LIKE COACH PASTERNAK SAID...

ANYWAY, THANKS FOR BEING SUCH A GOOD SPORT AND EVERYTHING...

DID YOU SEE THAT? WHAT THE FUCK IS THAT SUPPOSED TO MEAN?
WHO CARES? I COULDN'T CARE LESS IF THOSE PEOPLE LIKE ME OR NOT.

I DON'T GIVE A SHIT IF YOU LIKE ME, BUT YOU DAMN WELL BETTER SHOW SOME RESPECT!

YOU LIKE THIS?
YEAH.

MAN, YOU'RE A REAL SQUARE!
SO WHAT.

THAT'S OKAY-- I LIKE OLD MUSIC, TOO. AT LEAST YOU DON'T HAVE TO TAKE DRUGS TO UNDERSTAND IT.
ANDY!?

ANDY, WHERE IS YOUR GRANDFATHER?
I DUNNO... ISN'T HE IN HIS ROOM?

5.

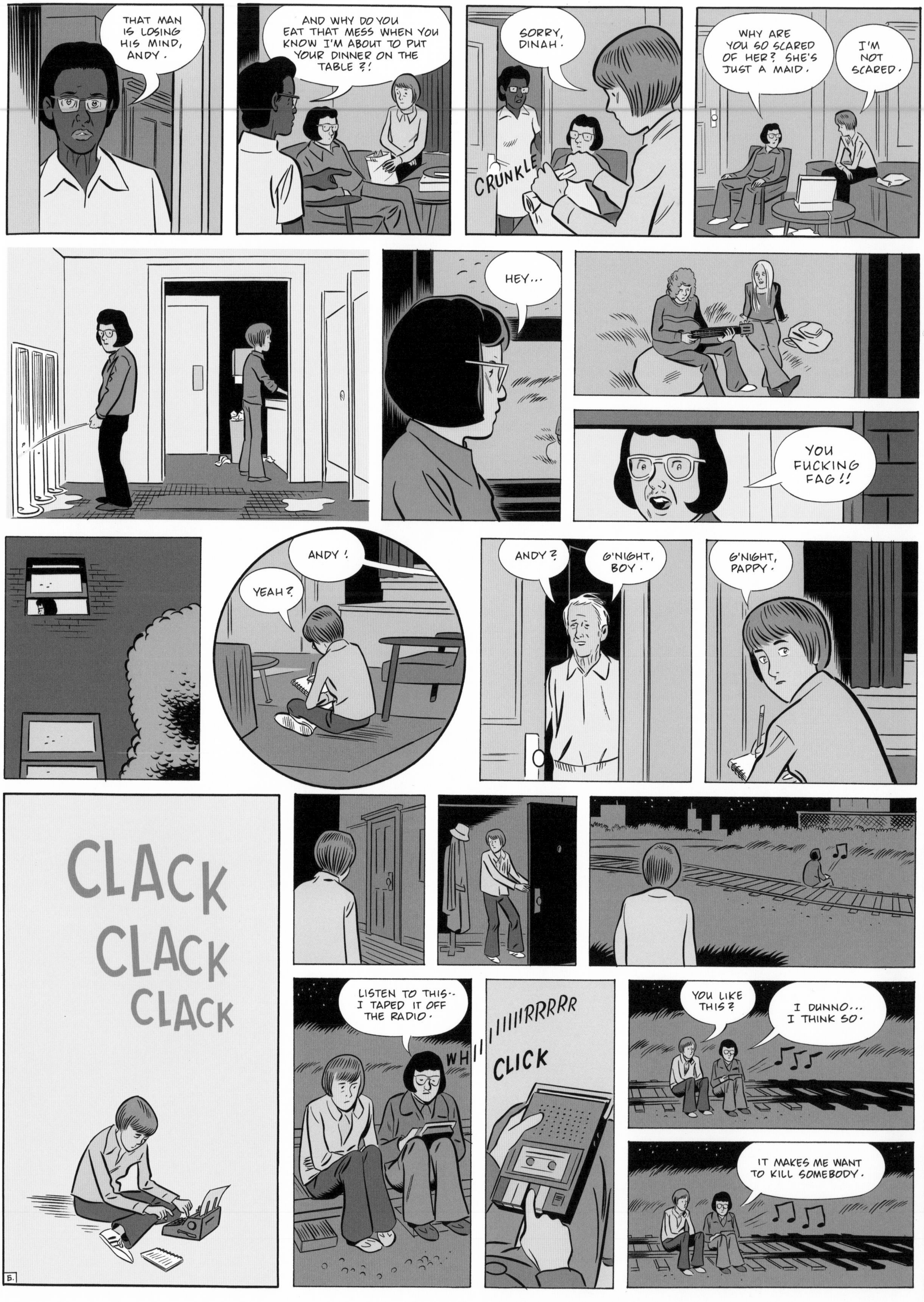
THAT MAN IS LOSING HIS MIND, ANDY.
AND WHY DO YOU EAT THAT MESS WHEN YOU KNOW I'M ABOUT TO PUT YOUR DINNER ON THE TABLE ?!
SORRY, DINAH.
CRUNKLE
WHY ARE YOU SO SCARED OF HER? SHE'S JUST A MAID.
I'M NOT SCARED.
HEY...
YOU FUCKING FAG !!
ANDY !
YEAH ?
ANDY ?
G'NIGHT, BOY.
G'NIGHT, PAPPY.
CLACK
CLACK
CLACK
LISTEN TO THIS.. I TAPED IT OFF THE RADIO.
WHIIIIIIIRRRRR
CLICK
YOU LIKE THIS ?
I DUNNO... I THINK SO.
IT MAKES ME WANT TO KILL SOMEBODY.

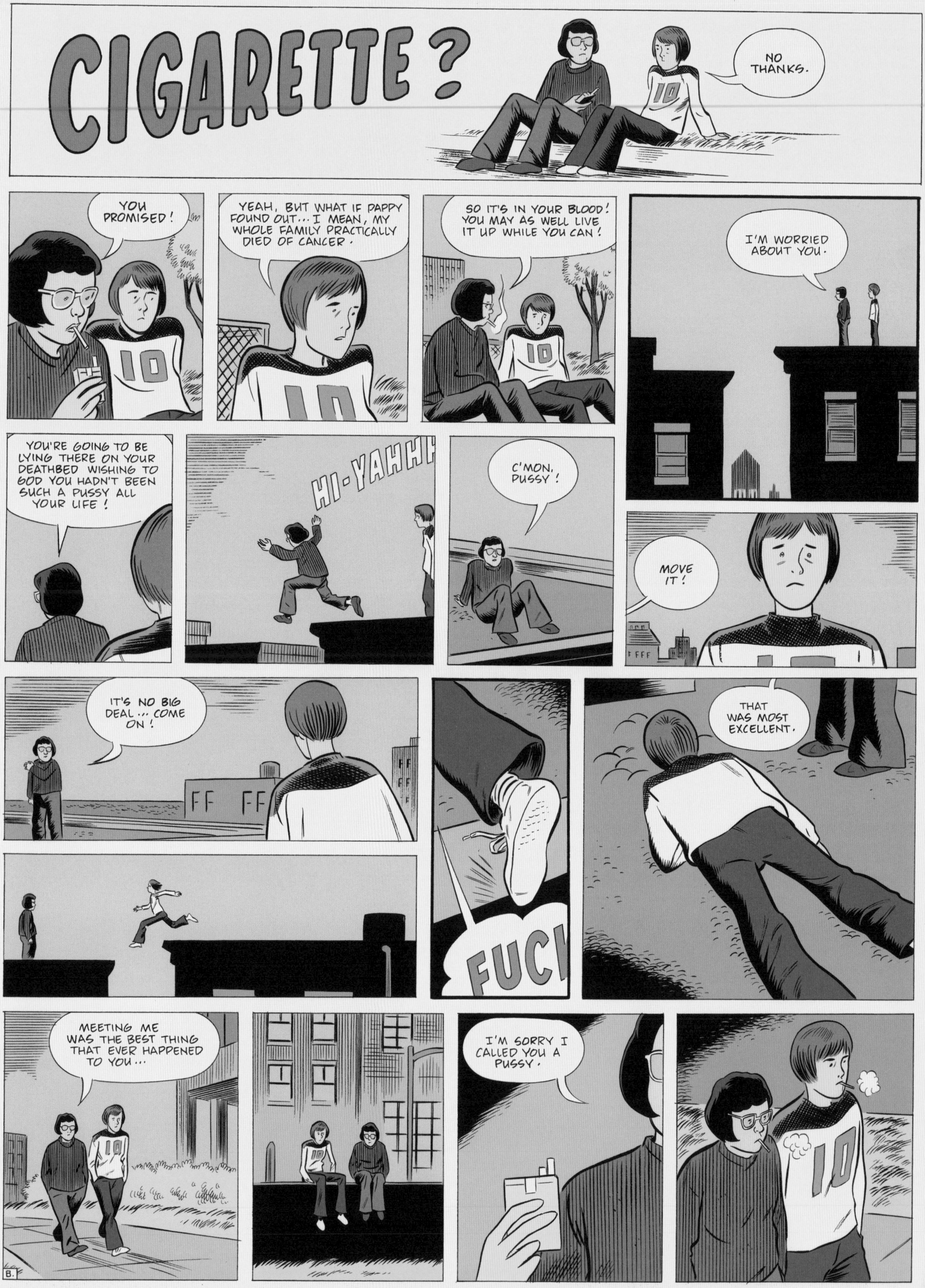
CIGARETTE?
NO THANKS.
YOU PROMISED!
YEAH, BUT WHAT IF PAPPY FOUND OUT... I MEAN, MY WHOLE FAMILY PRACTICALLY DIED OF CANCER.
SO IT'S IN YOUR BLOOD! YOU MAY AS WELL LIVE IT UP WHILE YOU CAN!
I'M WORRIED ABOUT YOU.
YOU'RE GOING TO BE LYING THERE ON YOUR DEATHBED WISHING TO GOD YOU HADN'T BEEN SUCH A PUSSY ALL YOUR LIFE!
HI-YAHHH
C'MON, PUSSY!
MOVE IT!
IT'S NO BIG DEAL... COME ON!
FUCI
THAT WAS MOST EXCELLENT.
MEETING ME WAS THE BEST THING THAT EVER HAPPENED TO YOU...
I'M SORRY I CALLED YOU A PUSSY.
B.

INCREDIBLE

9.

THE NEXT DAY

BOY, I HAD A PRETTY WEIRD NIGHT.

LOOK, THERE'S SOMETHING GOING DOWN TODAY AND I MAY NEED YOUR HELP.

I'VE HAD IT WITH THAT FUCKING ASSHOLE! TODAY IS THE DAY I TAKE HIM OUT!

EVERY MOLECULE HAD BEEN DRAINED OF ENERGY. I COULD BARELY SUMMON THE STRENGTH TO BREATHE.

IT OCCURRED TO ME THAT LOUIE HAD PUT DRUGS IN MY CIGARETTE, BUT THAT DIDN'T REALLY MAKE SENSE...

WHO, STOOB?

FUCK YEAH, STOOB!

AND WHAT AM I SUPPOSED TO DO?

JUST KEEP YOUR EAR TO THE GROUND.

DO YOU HAVE ENGLISH FIRST PERIOD?

NO, MATH.

CAN I BORROW YOUR ENGLISH BOOK?

WHY?

HEY, I GOT SOMETHING FOR YOU.

HAIR OF THE DOG.

WHAT'S THAT SUPPOSED TO MEAN?

YOU'RE SURE YOU WANT TO DO THIS?

FUCK YOU!

THE REST OF THE DAY WENT BY LIKE A DREAM... I NEVER REALLY FELT NORMAL ALL DAY.

I EVEN RAISED MY HAND IN SOCIAL STUDIES, JUST TO FREAK MR. BILLINGS OUT.

WHEN LOUIE DITCHED GYM I THOUGHT MAYBE HE WAS GOING TO WIMP OUT; NOT THAT HE WAS A CHICKEN OR ANYTHING... I ALSO WONDERED IF STOOB EVEN KNEW ABOUT THE FIGHT.

LATER, I TRIED TO IMAGINE HOW HARD COACH PASTERNAK WOULD SHIT IF HE SAW ME LIFT UP A CAR!

OKAY, I'M GONNA COUNT TO FIVE...

FUCK YOU!

ONE.

YOU DICK-SUCKING PIECE OF SHIT!

TWO.

THREE.

BEFORE LOUIE, I REALLY ONLY HAD ONE FRIEND. HIS NAME WAS CRAIG JONES AND HE WAS TOTALLY INTO HOT WHEELS.

SIX...

HE WAS MY BEST FRIEND FOR ALMOST THREE YEARS AND THEN SOMETHING HAPPENED. I HATE TO EVEN THINK ABOUT IT.

10.

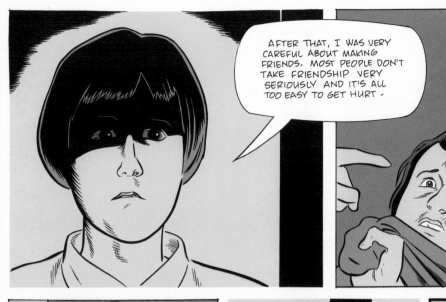

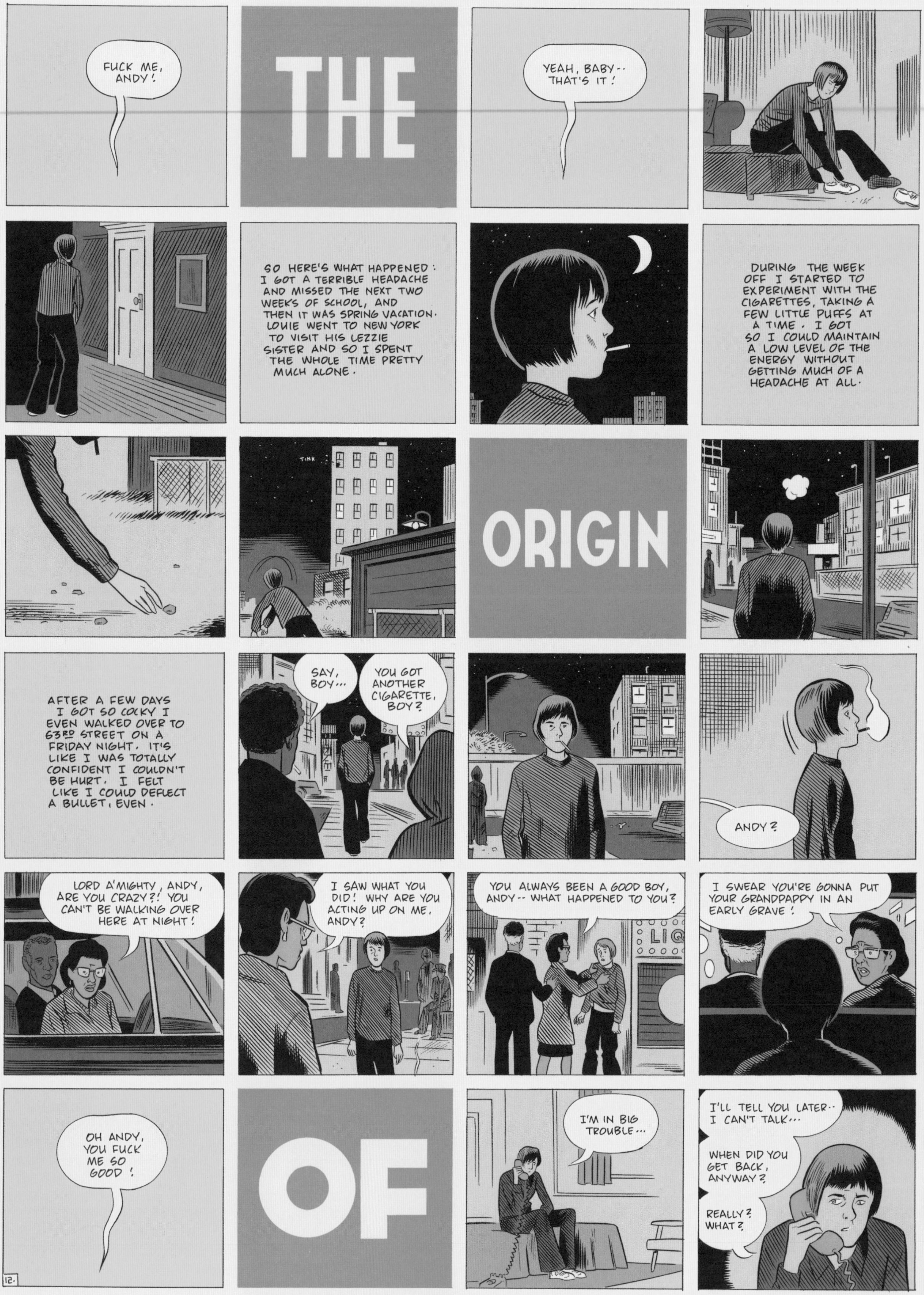
FUCK ME, ANDY!
THE
YEAH, BABY-- THAT'S IT!
SO HERE'S WHAT HAPPENED: I GOT A TERRIBLE HEADACHE AND MISSED THE NEXT TWO WEEKS OF SCHOOL, AND THEN IT WAS SPRING VACATION. LOUIE WENT TO NEW YORK TO VISIT HIS LEZZIE SISTER AND SO I SPENT THE WHOLE TIME PRETTY MUCH ALONE.
DURING THE WEEK OFF I STARTED TO EXPERIMENT WITH THE CIGARETTES, TAKING A FEW LITTLE PUFFS AT A TIME. I GOT SO I COULD MAINTAIN A LOW LEVEL OF THE ENERGY WITHOUT GETTING MUCH OF A HEADACHE AT ALL.
TINK
ORIGIN
AFTER A FEW DAYS I GOT SO COCKY I EVEN WALKED OVER TO 63RD STREET ON A FRIDAY NIGHT. IT'S LIKE I WAS TOTALLY CONFIDENT I COULDN'T BE HURT. I FELT LIKE I COULD DEFLECT A BULLET, EVEN.
SAY, BOY...
YOU GOT ANOTHER CIGARETTE, BOY?
ANDY?
LORD A'MIGHTY, ANDY, ARE YOU CRAZY?! YOU CAN'T BE WALKING OVER HERE AT NIGHT!
I SAW WHAT YOU DID! WHY ARE YOU ACTING UP ON ME, ANDY?
YOU ALWAYS BEEN A GOOD BOY, ANDY-- WHAT HAPPENED TO YOU?
LIQ
I SWEAR YOU'RE GONNA PUT YOUR GRANDPAPPY IN AN EARLY GRAVE!
OH ANDY, YOU FUCK ME SO GOOD!
OF
I'M IN BIG TROUBLE...
I'LL TELL YOU LATER-- I CAN'T TALK...
WHEN DID YOU GET BACK, ANYWAY?
REALLY? WHAT?
12.

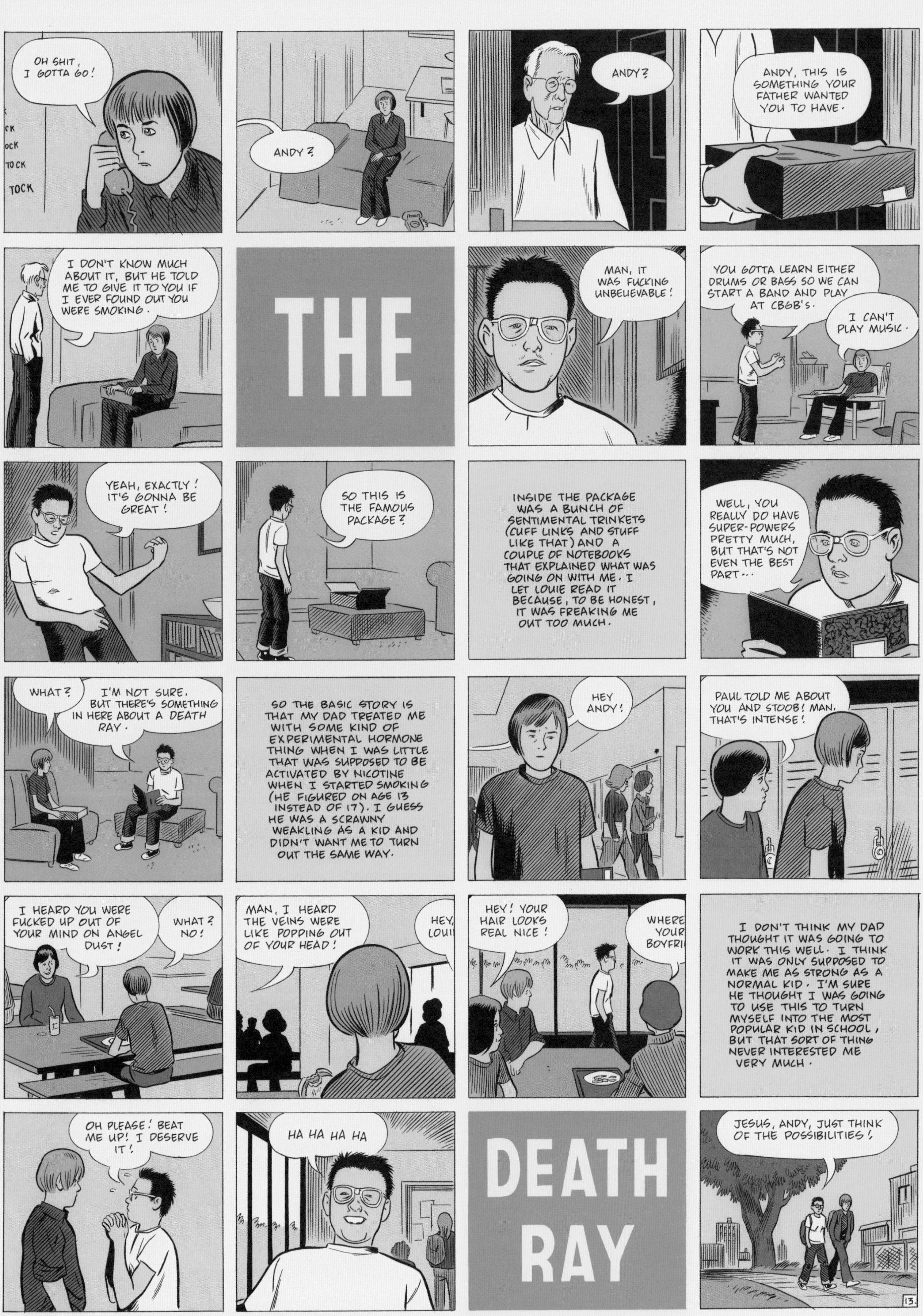
OH SHIT, I GOTTA GO!
CK
OCK
TOCK
TOCK
ANDY?
ANDY?
ANDY, THIS IS SOMETHING YOUR FATHER WANTED YOU TO HAVE.
I DON'T KNOW MUCH ABOUT IT, BUT HE TOLD ME TO GIVE IT TO YOU IF I EVER FOUND OUT YOU WERE SMOKING.
THE
MAN, IT WAS FUCKING UNBELIEVABLE!
YOU GOTTA LEARN EITHER DRUMS OR BASS SO WE CAN START A BAND AND PLAY AT CBGB'S.
I CAN'T PLAY MUSIC.
YEAH, EXACTLY! IT'S GONNA BE GREAT!
SO THIS IS THE FAMOUS PACKAGE?
INSIDE THE PACKAGE WAS A BUNCH OF SENTIMENTAL TRINKETS (CUFF LINKS AND STUFF LIKE THAT) AND A COUPLE OF NOTEBOOKS THAT EXPLAINED WHAT WAS GOING ON WITH ME. I LET LOUIE READ IT BECAUSE, TO BE HONEST, IT WAS FREAKING ME OUT TOO MUCH.
WELL, YOU REALLY DO HAVE SUPER-POWERS PRETTY MUCH, BUT THAT'S NOT EVEN THE BEST PART...
WHAT?
I'M NOT SURE. BUT THERE'S SOMETHING IN HERE ABOUT A DEATH RAY.
SO THE BASIC STORY IS THAT MY DAD TREATED ME WITH SOME KIND OF EXPERIMENTAL HORMONE THING WHEN I WAS LITTLE THAT WAS SUPPOSED TO BE ACTIVATED BY NICOTINE WHEN I STARTED SMOKING (HE FIGURED ON AGE 13 INSTEAD OF 17). I GUESS HE WAS A SCRAWNY WEAKLING AS A KID AND DIDN'T WANT ME TO TURN OUT THE SAME WAY.
HEY ANDY!
PAUL TOLD ME ABOUT YOU AND STOOB! MAN, THAT'S INTENSE!
I HEARD YOU WERE FUCKED UP OUT OF YOUR MIND ON ANGEL DUST!
WHAT? NO!
MAN, I HEARD THE VEINS WERE LIKE POPPING OUT OF YOUR HEAD!
HEY, LOUI
HEY! YOUR HAIR LOOKS REAL NICE!
WHERE YOUR BOYFRI
I DON'T THINK MY DAD THOUGHT IT WAS GOING TO WORK THIS WELL. I THINK IT WAS ONLY SUPPOSED TO MAKE ME AS STRONG AS A NORMAL KID. I'M SURE HE THOUGHT I WAS GOING TO USE THIS TO TURN MYSELF INTO THE MOST POPULAR KID IN SCHOOL, BUT THAT SORT OF THING NEVER INTERESTED ME VERY MUCH.
OH PLEASE! BEAT ME UP! I DESERVE IT!
HA HA HA HA
DEATH RAY
JESUS, ANDY, JUST THINK OF THE POSSIBILITIES!

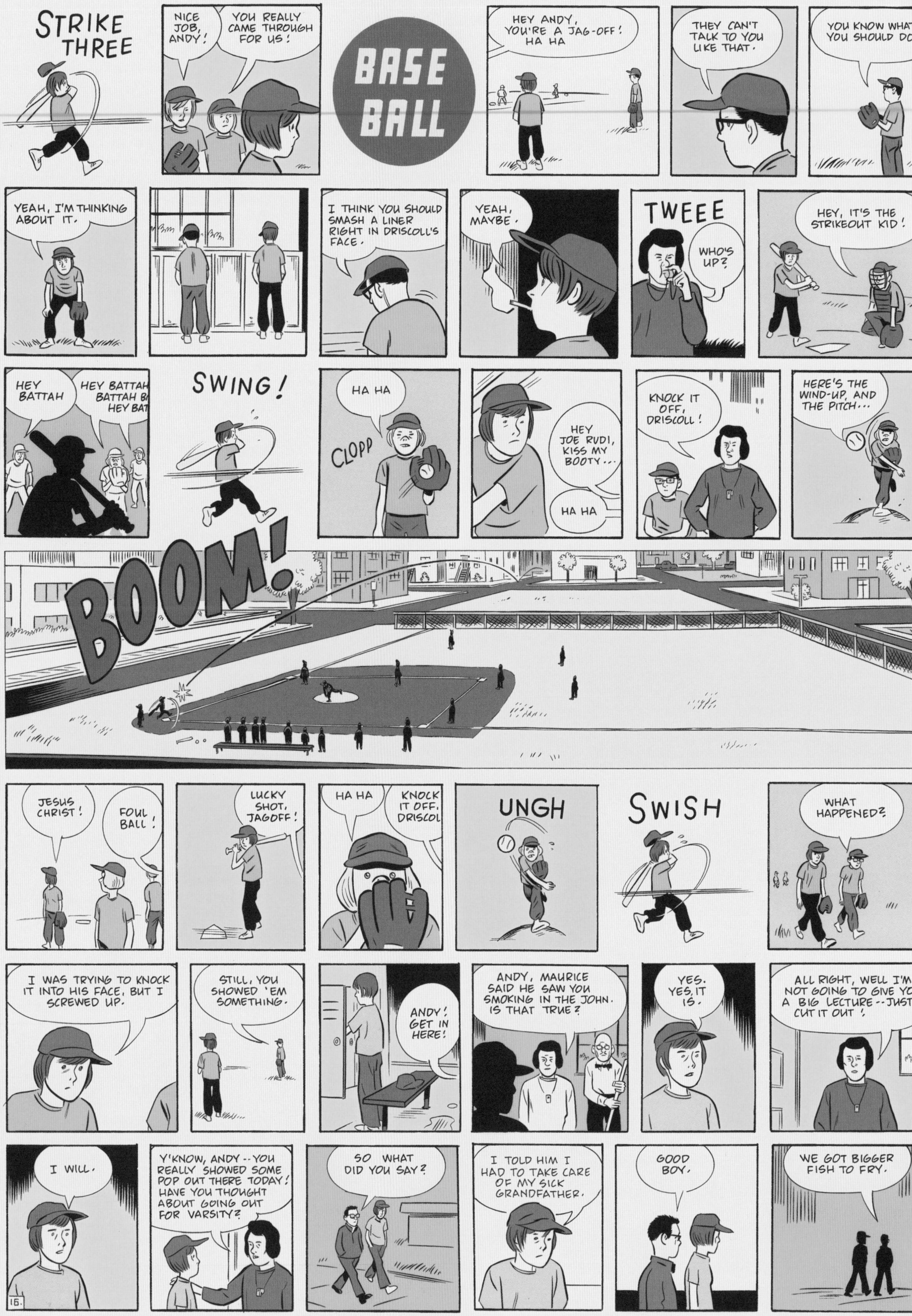
STRIKE THREE
NICE JOB, ANDY!
YOU REALLY CAME THROUGH FOR US!
BASE BALL
HEY ANDY, YOU'RE A JAG-OFF! HA HA
THEY CAN'T TALK TO YOU LIKE THAT.
YOU KNOW WHAT YOU SHOULD DO?
YEAH, I'M THINKING ABOUT IT.
I THINK YOU SHOULD SMASH A LINER RIGHT IN DRISCOLL'S FACE.
YEAH, MAYBE.
TWEEE
WHO'S UP?
HEY, IT'S THE STRIKEOUT KID!
HEY BATTAH
HEY BATTAH BATTAH B HEY BAT
SWING!
HA HA
CLOPP
KNOCK IT OFF, DRISCOLL!
HEY JOE RUDI, KISS MY BOOTY...
HA HA
HERE'S THE WIND-UP, AND THE PITCH...
BOOM!
JESUS CHRIST!
FOUL BALL!
LUCKY SHOT, JAGOFF!
HA HA
KNOCK IT OFF, DRISCOL
UNGH
SWISH
WHAT HAPPENED?
I WAS TRYING TO KNOCK IT INTO HIS FACE. BUT I SCREWED UP.
STILL, YOU SHOWED 'EM SOMETHING.
ANDY! GET IN HERE!
ANDY, MAURICE SAID HE SAW YOU SMOKING IN THE JOHN. IS THAT TRUE?
YES. YES, IT IS.
ALL RIGHT, WELL I'M NOT GOING TO GIVE YOU A BIG LECTURE -- JUST CUT IT OUT!
I WILL.
Y'KNOW, ANDY -- YOU REALLY SHOWED SOME POP OUT THERE TODAY! HAVE YOU THOUGHT ABOUT GOING OUT FOR VARSITY?
SO WHAT DID YOU SAY?
I TOLD HIM I HAD TO TAKE CARE OF MY SICK GRANDFATHER.
GOOD BOY.
WE GOT BIGGER FISH TO FRY.

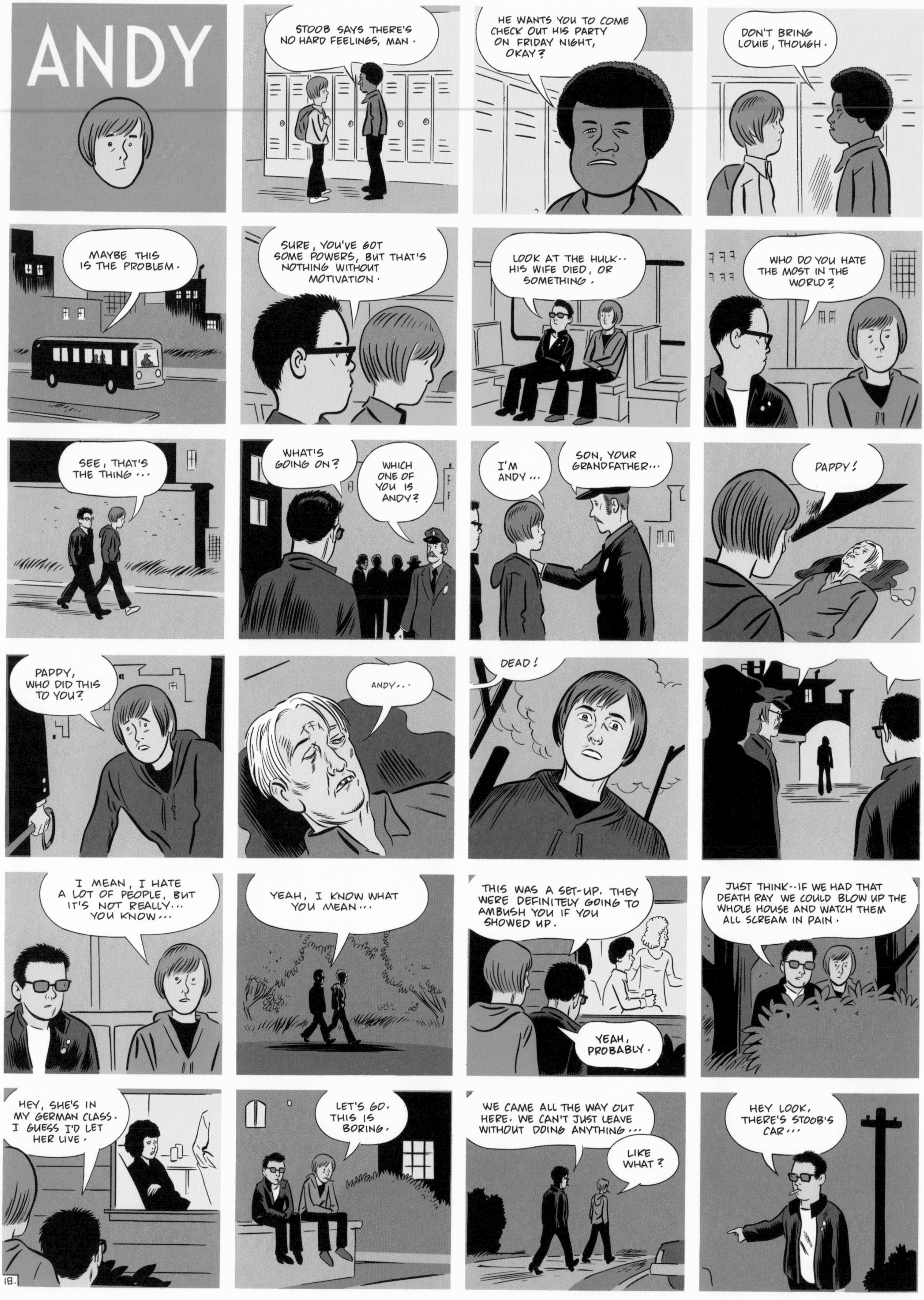
ANDY
STOOB SAYS THERE'S NO HARD FEELINGS, MAN.
HE WANTS YOU TO COME CHECK OUT HIS PARTY ON FRIDAY NIGHT, OKAY?
DON'T BRING LOUIE, THOUGH.
MAYBE THIS IS THE PROBLEM.
SURE, YOU'VE GOT SOME POWERS, BUT THAT'S NOTHING WITHOUT MOTIVATION.
LOOK AT THE HULK.. HIS WIFE DIED, OR SOMETHING.
WHO DO YOU HATE THE MOST IN THE WORLD?
SEE, THAT'S THE THING...
WHAT'S GOING ON?
WHICH ONE OF YOU IS ANDY?
I'M ANDY...
SON, YOUR GRANDFATHER...
PAPPY!
PAPPY, WHO DID THIS TO YOU?
ANDY...
DEAD!
I MEAN, I HATE A LOT OF PEOPLE, BUT IT'S NOT REALLY... YOU KNOW...
YEAH, I KNOW WHAT YOU MEAN...
THIS WAS A SET-UP. THEY WERE DEFINITELY GOING TO AMBUSH YOU IF YOU SHOWED UP.
YEAH, PROBABLY.
JUST THINK--IF WE HAD THAT DEATH RAY WE COULD BLOW UP THE WHOLE HOUSE AND WATCH THEM ALL SCREAM IN PAIN.
HEY, SHE'S IN MY GERMAN CLASS. I GUESS I'D LET HER LIVE.
LET'S GO. THIS IS BORING.
WE CAME ALL THE WAY OUT HERE. WE CAN'T JUST LEAVE WITHOUT DOING ANYTHING...
LIKE WHAT?
HEY LOOK, THERE'S STOOB'S CAR...
18.

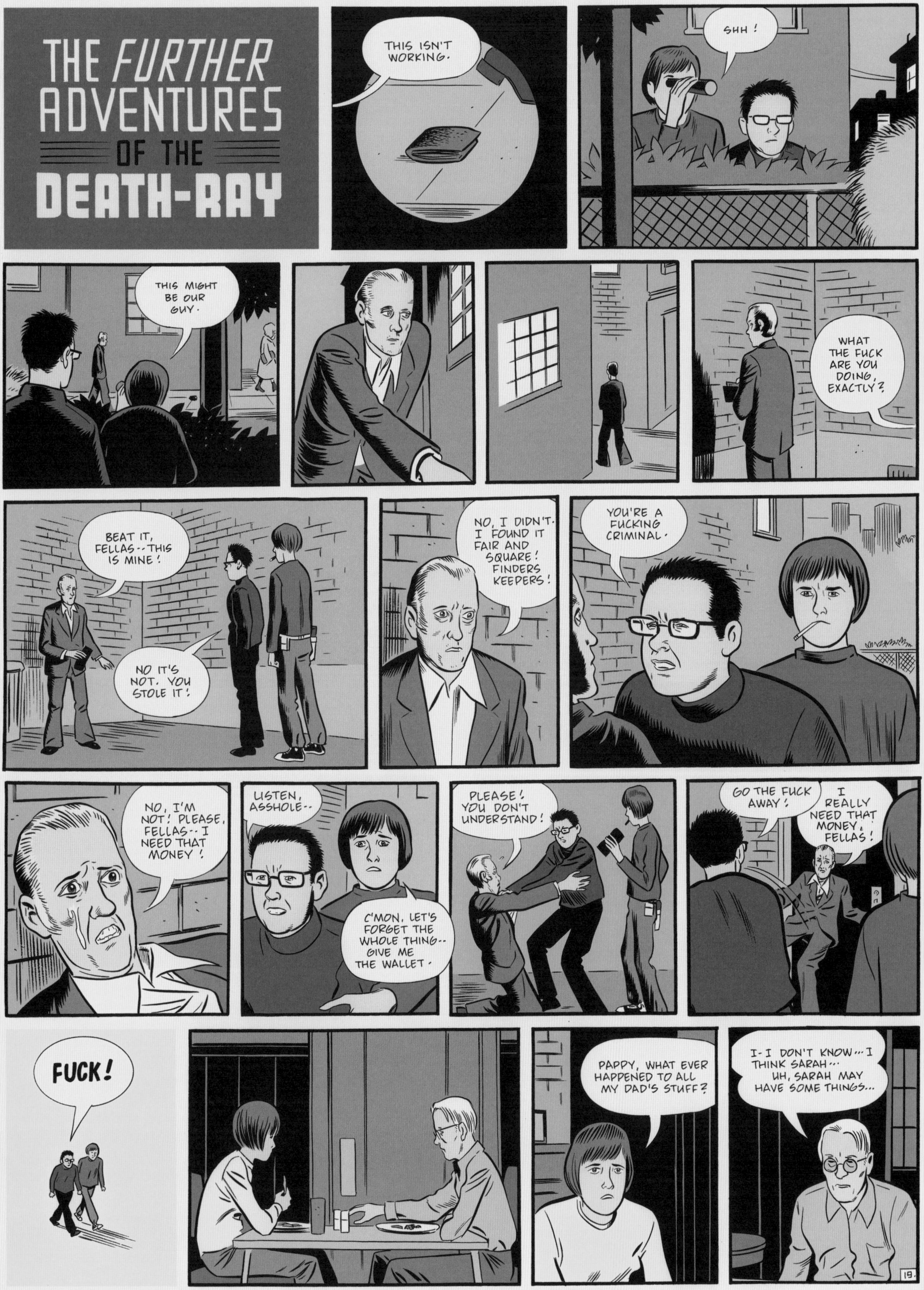
THE FURTHER ADVENTURES OF THE DEATH-RAY
THIS ISN'T WORKING.
SHH!
THIS MIGHT BE OUR GUY.
WHAT THE FUCK ARE YOU DOING, EXACTLY?
BEAT IT, FELLAS-- THIS IS MINE!
NO IT'S NOT. YOU STOLE IT!
NO, I DIDN'T. I FOUND IT FAIR AND SQUARE! FINDERS KEEPERS!
YOU'RE A FUCKING CRIMINAL.
NO, I'M NOT! PLEASE, FELLAS-- I NEED THAT MONEY!
LISTEN, ASSHOLE--
C'MON, LET'S FORGET THE WHOLE THING-- GIVE ME THE WALLET.
PLEASE! YOU DON'T UNDERSTAND!
GO THE FUCK AWAY!
I REALLY NEED THAT MONEY, FELLAS!
FUCK!
PAPPY, WHAT EVER HAPPENED TO ALL MY DAD'S STUFF?
I- I DON'T KNOW... I THINK SARAH... UH, SARAH MAY HAVE SOME THINGS...

21.

AFTER DAD DIED I WAS SUPPOSED TO GO LIVE WITH HER, BUT LUCKILY I WAS ABLE TO SCAM THE CHILD PSYCHOLOGIST INTO LETTING ME STAY AT HOME WITH PAPPY.

ANYWAY, SHE SAID THE PACKAGE WAS IN THE MAIL...YEAH, AND I WON'T COME IN YOUR MOUTH (THAT'S AN OLD GEORGE CARLIN JOKE, I THINK).

I LIKED AUNT DELIA OKAY, EXCEPT SHE ALWAYS KIND OF MADE ME FEEL LIKE A PATHETIC TURD. SHE REALLY DID NOT GET ME AT ALL.

STILL, I HAVE TO SAY I THINK I COME FROM A PRETTY GREAT FAMILY. I MEAN, JUST THINK ABOUT WHAT MY DAD DID FOR ME. WHAT DAD HAS EVER DONE ANYTHING LIKE THAT BEFORE?

AND PAPPY, TOO... HE WAS ALWAYS GREAT TO ME... I JUST WISH...

I'VE BEEN THINKING A LOT LATELY ABOUT HOW MUCH STUFF WE TAKE FOR GRANTED. WE'RE SO LUCKY TO LIVE IN THE MODERN WORLD. I MEAN, IF YOU WERE BORN IN UNCIVILIZED TIMES, YOU'D SPEND ALL DAY LOOKING FOR GRUBS AND THEN YOU'D DIE IN PAIN AT AGE TWENTY.

REALLY, WE SHOULD ALL BE SO THANKFUL FOR OUR ANCESTORS IN THE HUMAN RACE.

THAT'S WHY I FEEL I HAVE TO DO MY PART, HOWEVER SMALL, TO HELP OUT HUMANITY, OR AT LEAST THE GOOD, DECENT MEMBERS OF SOCIETY.

IT'S NOT EASY, THOUGH...AND TO BE HONEST, A LOT OF THE TIME IT FEELS KIND OF LIKE HOMEWORK.

BUT SOMEBODY HAS TO IMPOSE SOME KIND OF STRUCTURE ON THE WORLD, I GUESS. OTHERWISE EVERYTHING WOULD JUST FALL APART, WOULDN'T IT?

TARGET PRACTICE

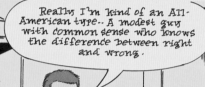

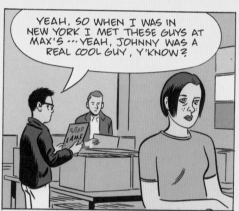

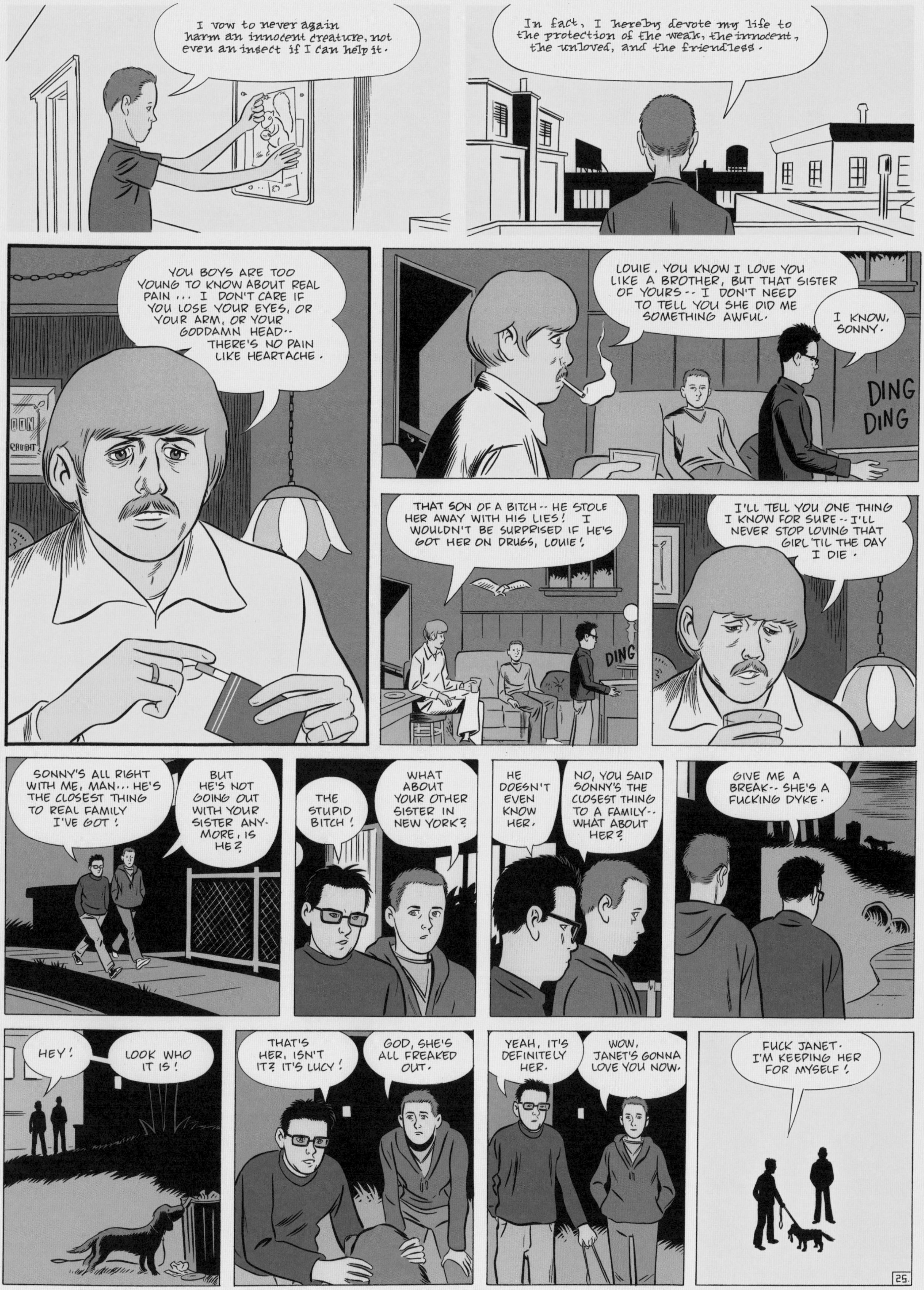
I vow to never again harm an innocent creature, not even an insect if I can help it.
In fact, I hereby devote my life to the protection of the weak, the innocent, the unloved, and the friendless.
YOU BOYS ARE TOO YOUNG TO KNOW ABOUT REAL PAIN... I DON'T CARE IF YOU LOSE YOUR EYES, OR YOUR ARM, OR YOUR GODDAMN HEAD-- THERE'S NO PAIN LIKE HEARTACHE.
LOUIE, YOU KNOW I LOVE YOU LIKE A BROTHER, BUT THAT SISTER OF YOURS-- I DON'T NEED TO TELL YOU SHE DID ME SOMETHING AWFUL.
I KNOW, SONNY.
DING DING
THAT SON OF A BITCH-- HE STOLE HER AWAY WITH HIS LIES! I WOULDN'T BE SURPRISED IF HE'S GOT HER ON DRUGS, LOUIE!
DING
I'LL TELL YOU ONE THING I KNOW FOR SURE-- I'LL NEVER STOP LOVING THAT GIRL 'TIL THE DAY I DIE.
SONNY'S ALL RIGHT WITH ME, MAN... HE'S THE CLOSEST THING TO REAL FAMILY I'VE GOT!
BUT HE'S NOT GOING OUT WITH YOUR SISTER ANYMORE, IS HE?
THE STUPID BITCH!
WHAT ABOUT YOUR OTHER SISTER IN NEW YORK?
HE DOESN'T EVEN KNOW HER.
NO, YOU SAID SONNY'S THE CLOSEST THING TO A FAMILY-- WHAT ABOUT HER?
GIVE ME A BREAK-- SHE'S A FUCKING DYKE.
HEY!
LOOK WHO IT IS!
THAT'S HER, ISN'T IT? IT'S LUCY!
GOD, SHE'S ALL FREAKED OUT.
YEAH, IT'S DEFINITELY HER.
WOW, JANET'S GONNA LOVE YOU NOW.
FUCK JANET. I'M KEEPING HER FOR MYSELF!

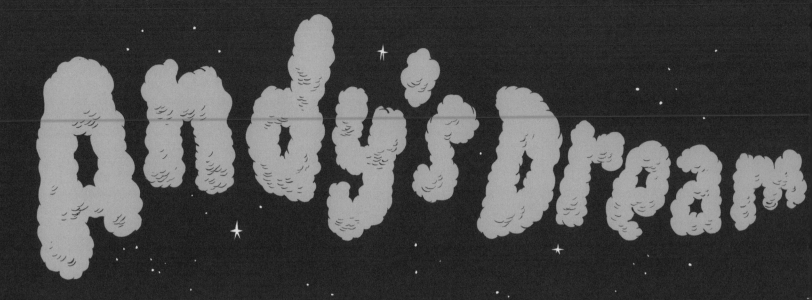

There was this tree with these big white berries growing on it, and as soon as a person ate one they would start to disappear.

This process seemed to be both physically painful and super-terrifying.

I was so scared of the tree, which I guess was supposed to be in my back yard, that I didn't even want to go outside.

I stayed in my room for a long time and it seemed pretty safe until I started to notice these weird little clouds floating up around the ceiling. I was able to get rid of them by waving a broom around, but after a few hours they came back even stronger.

I went to make a break for it, but outside the door was pure whiteness. It filled up the room and blanked it out. I've never been so scared.

I woke up totally drenched. No matter what I did, I couldn't get away from the nothingness.

Later that night I had another dream. In this one I was having sex with my housekeeper.

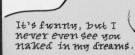

It's funny, but I never even see you naked in my dreams.

I guess my brain has too much respect for you.

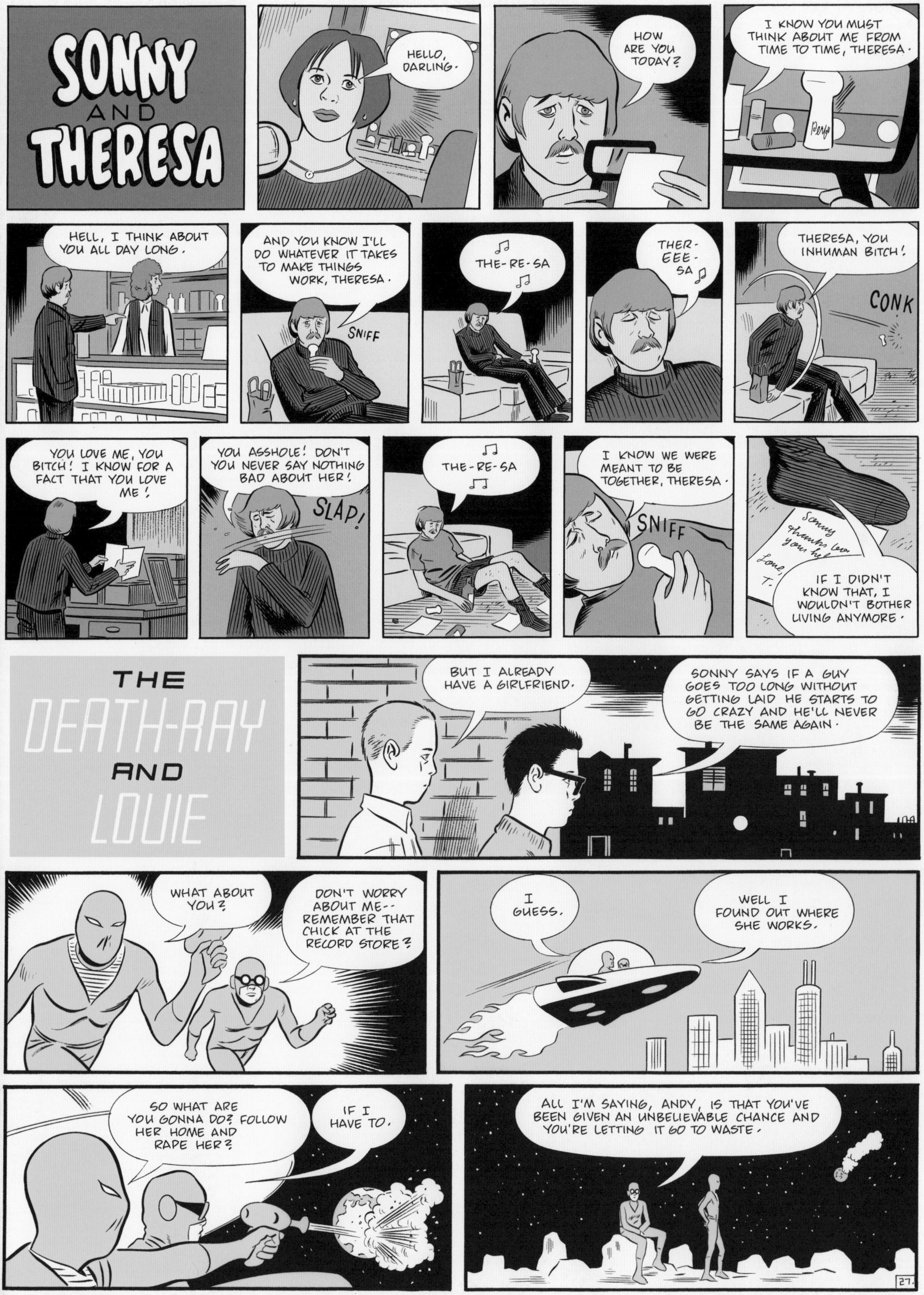
SONNY AND THERESA
HELLO, DARLING.
HOW ARE YOU TODAY?
I KNOW YOU MUST THINK ABOUT ME FROM TIME TO TIME, THERESA.
HELL, I THINK ABOUT YOU ALL DAY LONG.
AND YOU KNOW I'LL DO WHATEVER IT TAKES TO MAKE THINGS WORK, THERESA.
SNIFF
♫ THE-RE-SA ♫
THER-EEE-SA ♫
THERESA, YOU INHUMAN BITCH!
CONK
YOU LOVE ME, YOU BITCH! I KNOW FOR A FACT THAT YOU LOVE ME!
YOU ASSHOLE! DON'T YOU NEVER SAY NOTHING BAD ABOUT HER!
SLAP!
♫ THE-RE-SA ♫
I KNOW WE WERE MEANT TO BE TOGETHER, THERESA.
SNIFF
IF I DIDN'T KNOW THAT, I WOULDN'T BOTHER LIVING ANYMORE.
THE DEATH-RAY AND LOUIE
BUT I ALREADY HAVE A GIRLFRIEND.
SONNY SAYS IF A GUY GOES TOO LONG WITHOUT GETTING LAID HE STARTS TO GO CRAZY AND HE'LL NEVER BE THE SAME AGAIN.
WHAT ABOUT YOU?
DON'T WORRY ABOUT ME-- REMEMBER THAT CHICK AT THE RECORD STORE?
I GUESS.
WELL I FOUND OUT WHERE SHE WORKS.
SO WHAT ARE YOU GONNA DO? FOLLOW HER HOME AND RAPE HER?
IF I HAVE TO.
ALL I'M SAYING, ANDY, IS THAT YOU'VE BEEN GIVEN AN UNBELIEVABLE CHANCE AND YOU'RE LETTING IT GO TO WASTE.
27.

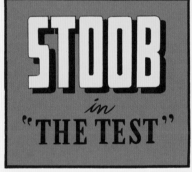

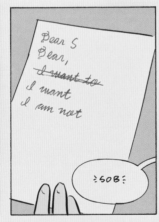

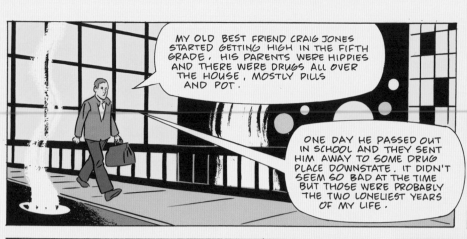

MY OLD BEST FRIEND CRAIG JONES STARTED GETTING HIGH IN THE FIFTH GRADE. HIS PARENTS WERE HIPPIES AND THERE WERE DRUGS ALL OVER THE HOUSE, MOSTLY PILLS AND POT.

ONE DAY HE PASSED OUT IN SCHOOL AND THEY SENT HIM AWAY TO SOME DRUG PLACE DOWNSTATE. IT DIDN'T SEEM SO BAD AT THE TIME BUT THOSE WERE PROBABLY THE TWO LONELIEST YEARS OF MY LIFE.

WHEN HE CAME BACK HE WAS ALL OF A SUDDEN REALLY POPULAR, BUT HE STILL USED TO COME OVER AND HANG OUT WITH ME. WE WOULD JUST WATCH TV OR PLAY NERF BASKETBALL AND IT WAS PRETTY MUCH LIKE OLD TIMES.

ONE DAY AFTER SCHOOL, DINAH CAUGHT HIM GOING THROUGH HER PURSE. HE HAD STOLEN A TON OF OUR STUFF IT TURNED OUT, INCLUDING SOME OF PAPPY'S PILLS.

I WOULD STILL SEE HIM AROUND SCHOOL AFTER THAT, BUT HE WAS PART OF A WHOLE DIFFERENT CROWD. A FEW YEARS LATER HE DROPPED OUT AND I NEVER SAW HIM AGAIN.

WE'RE THE COOLEST GUYS IN THE WORLD.

MAYBE SO.

IT'S NOT AN OPINION, IT'S A FACT.

DID YOU TELL SONNY ABOUT THE GUN?

NO WAY. I'M TOTALLY LOYAL TO YOU, ANDY.

NO WAY IN HELL.

AND ANYWAY, WE'RE NOT DOING IT FOR SONNY, WE'RE DOING IT FOR AMERICA!

Y'KNOW?

NOBODY WILL EVER KNOW A THING, ANDY.

FOR ALL THEY KNOW, HE JUST MOVED AWAY.

FOR ALL THEY KNOW, HE JUST WENT ON VACATION. THEY'LL NEVER--

POP

30.

THE UNTHINKABLE

FEETS DON'T FAIL ME NOW!

YOU'D THINK SOMETHING LIKE THAT WOULD FREAK ME OUT, BUT I HARDLY GAVE IT ANOTHER THOUGHT. I GUESS I'M GROWING UP. I MEAN, ADULTS HAVE TO DEAL WITH TOUGH DECISIONS EVERY DAY. NOT THAT IT'S SOMETHING I TAKE LIGHTLY, AND I HOPE TO GOD I NEVER HAVE TO DO IT AGAIN EVER, BUT...

I DIDN'T THINK HE HAD IT IN HIM. I WAS JUST-- I DON'T KNOW, I JUST DIDN'T EXPECT IT. I MEAN, HE WAS MORE UPSET ABOUT THE CHIPMUNK! I GUESS I SHOULD BE GLAD HE'S MY FRIEND, BUT JESUS CHRIST, ANDY!

THANKS, DUDE.

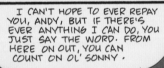

ANDY, I DON'T KNOW THE WHOLE STORY-- I'M PRETTY SURE I DON'T WANT TO KNOW...

I CAN'T HOPE TO EVER REPAY YOU, ANDY, BUT IF THERE'S EVER ANYTHING I CAN DO, YOU JUST SAY THE WORD. FROM HERE ON OUT, YOU CAN COUNT ON OL' SONNY.

SO I'VE BEEN DOING SOME THINKING, ANDY...

'SCUSE ME, BOYS...

ANDY, BUDDY-- CAN I BORROW YOU FOR A SEC?

I MEAN IT, BUDDY.

SO I THINK WE SHOULD STASH THE GUN SOMEWHERE... Y'KNOW, JUST FOR A WHILE UNTIL WE FIGURE OUT WHAT WE'RE DOING.

LOOK, LOUIE-- I'M THE BOSS NOW.

OH, OKAY ANDY. WHATEVER YOU SAY.

SO WHO ARE YOU GONNA KILL NEXT?

WHAT'S THAT SUPPOSED TO MEAN?

NOTHING... I JUST THOUGHT...

31.

ANDY, WHERE HAVE YOU BEEN?

SORRY, DINAH... I WAS JUST...

ANDY, WE CAN'T BE LEAVING YOUR GRANDFATHER ALONE ANYMORE.

HE ALMOST BURNED THE DAMN HOUSE DOWN, ANDY! THERE'S WATER ALL OVER THE KITCHEN, AND EVERYTHING'S ALL MESSED UP!

YOU LISTEN, ANDY... YOU BETTER CALL UP YOUR AUNT DELIA TONIGHT... YOU ASK HER WHAT TO DO.

I HAVE TO GET A MOVE ON, ANDY... YOU CALL HER, HEAR?

OH, ANDY, WHAT'S GOING TO HAPPEN TO YOU?

I LOVE YOU, DINAH.

A WEEK AFTER WE TOOK CARE OF THERESA'S BOYFRIEND, LOUIE CALLED ME UP AND SAID, "YOU KNOW, C.J. WAS A FUCKING ASSHOLE, BUT HE DIDN'T DESERVE TO DIE. YOU DIDN'T EVEN KNOW THE GUY." THIS REALLY HIT ME. I MEAN, IT WAS HIS IDEA IN THE FIRST PLACE! THE COSTUME, THE ROOFTOP, EVERYTHING!

ANYWAY, THAT'S WHEN I DECIDED THAT I HAVE TO ALWAYS THINK FOR MYSELF, ONE HUNDRED PERCENT.

HELL, I'M A BIG BOY. I KNOW WHAT I'M DOING.

I DON'T NEED A GUY LIKE LOUIE TELLING ME HOW TO LIVE. I'M NOT THE ONE WHO NEEDS TO GROW UP!

JUST BECAUSE YOU'VE GOT A GIRLFRIEND DOESN'T MEAN YOU'RE A GODDAMN ADULT, LOUIE, SO STOP ACTING ALL SUPERIOR!

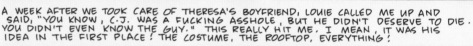

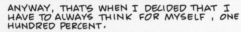

Dear Dusty (again)

I'm sorry I haven't written in so long, though I guess I shouldn't be. Did you know you haven't written me since that Christmas card?

Do you really love me at all? I hope so, though it would be better for you if you didn't.

I've been involved in something big. I can't talk about it right now, but you'll know everything some day.

If you ever get a package from me, DON'T OPEN IT. Put it in your closet and hide it away until you receive further instructions.

So how are you? I am fine. Actually, I feel kind of weird lately. I haven't been hanging out with Louie as much. He has a girlfriend now, so he's busy.

That's all for now. Why don't you write back to me soon, okay?

andy

P.S. Even if it's just a short note to tell me to stop bothering you.

LOUIE IN LOVE

ANDY, LOUIE

33.

34.

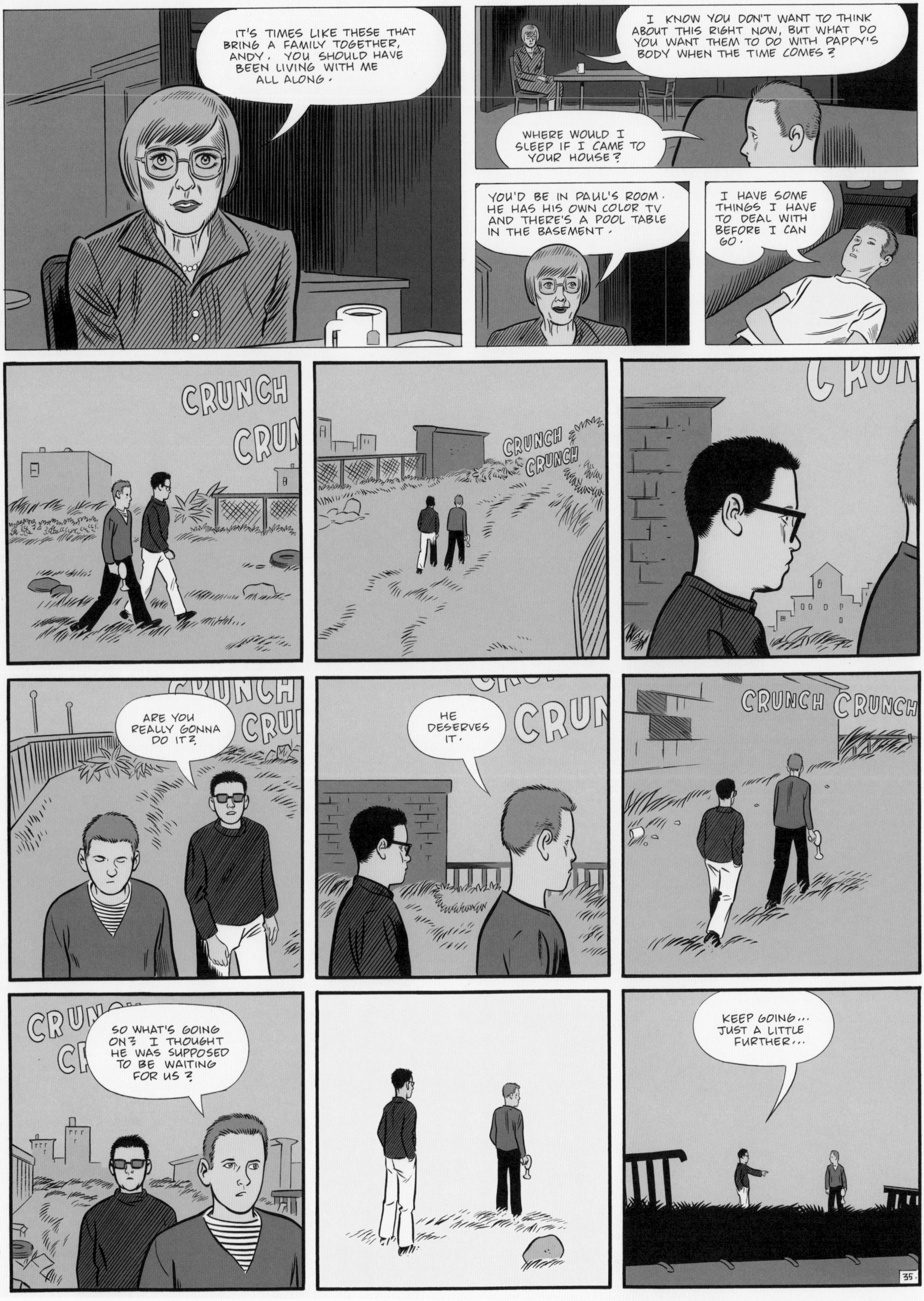
IT'S TIMES LIKE THESE THAT BRING A FAMILY TOGETHER, ANDY. YOU SHOULD HAVE BEEN LIVING WITH ME ALL ALONG.
I KNOW YOU DON'T WANT TO THINK ABOUT THIS RIGHT NOW, BUT WHAT DO YOU WANT THEM TO DO WITH PAPPY'S BODY WHEN THE TIME COMES?
WHERE WOULD I SLEEP IF I CAME TO YOUR HOUSE?
YOU'D BE IN PAUL'S ROOM. HE HAS HIS OWN COLOR TV AND THERE'S A POOL TABLE IN THE BASEMENT.
I HAVE SOME THINGS I HAVE TO DEAL WITH BEFORE I CAN GO.
CRUNCH
CRUN
CRUNCH
CRUNCH
CRUN
CRUNCH
CRU
ARE YOU REALLY GONNA DO IT?
CRUN
HE DESERVES IT.
CRUNCH CRUNCH
CRUN
SO WHAT'S GOING ON? I THOUGHT HE WAS SUPPOSED TO BE WAITING FOR US?
KEEP GOING... JUST A LITTLE FURTHER...

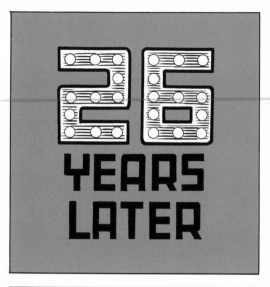

26 YEARS LATER

SO I WAS GOING TO TELL YOU ABOUT ALL THE TIMES I'VE FALLEN OFF THE WAGON...

I WAS GOOD FOR MANY YEARS. DIDN'T TOUCH TOBACCO AT ALL. IF SOMEONE GAVE ME GRIEF, I JUST STOOD THERE AND TOOK IT LIKE A MAN.

SO ONE DAY, THERE I WAS -- THIS IS AROUND THE TIME OF MY FIRST DIVORCE -- I'M IN THIS POLACK BAR ON THE WEST SIDE AND SOME DRUNK IS GIVING THE BARTENDER A HARD TIME WHILE HE AND HIS BUDDIES ARE TRYING TO WATCH A GAME.

NOTHING BIG, JUST BUGGING HIM, TRYING TO MAKE CONVERSATION.

LOOK, DUDE, I'M BUSY. WHY DON'T YOU GO SOMEWHERE ELSE?

I DON'T HAVE NOWHERE TO GO... LOOK, I'M NOT TRYING TO--. I JUST-- LOOK, I'M SORRY, MAN -- MY GRANDMOTHER DIED TODAY, Y'KNOW?

I DON'T GIVE A SHIT. WHO CARES? I'M TRYING TO WATCH THIS.

SO I SAY TO THE GUY NEXT TO ME, "HEY, HAVE YOU GOT A CIGARETTE?" I DIDN'T SMOKE IT RIGHT AWAY, THOUGH; I JUST WENT OUTSIDE AND WAITED.

BY THE TIME THE BARTENDER CLOSED UP I WAS STARTING TO FEEL A LITTLE SICK. IT HAD BEEN A LONG TIME.

STILL, I WAS ABLE TO DO SOME DAMAGE, AND I'LL BE DAMNED IF IT DIDN'T FEEL PRETTY GOOD.

A COUPLE WEEKS LATER I HAD ANOTHER SITUATION, AND ANOTHER A FEW WEEKS AFTER THAT. THERE'S ALWAYS SOME PRICK WHO NEEDS A LESSON. I NEVER LET IT GET OUT OF HAND, THOUGH, AND I NEVER EVEN THOUGHT ABOUT THE DEATH RAY.

HE WAS FRESH OUT OF THE ARMY AND WAS LIVING WITH HIS GIRLFRIEND, WHO SURE AS HELL DESERVED BETTER. I COULD HEAR HIM RAPING HER EVERY NIGHT. SHIT, THAT WAS REASON ENOUGH TO TAKE HIM DOWN.

I USED TO KEEP LUCY CHAINED TO THE FRONT PORCH. DIANNE ALWAYS STAYS INSIDE. ARMY-BOY HAD THIS VICIOUS PIT-BULL AND ONE DAY I CAME DOWNSTAIRS AND THERE WAS LUCY BLEEDING WITH A BIG BITE MARK ON HER NECK!

THAT NIGHT, I COULD HEAR HIM LAUGHING ABOUT IT -- HE THOUGHT IT WAS FUCKING HILARIOUS!

I KNEW WHAT I HAD TO DO, BUT I WASN'T SO FOOLISH AS TO THINK I COULD GO IT ALONE.

WELL LOOK WHO IT IS.

YOU DON'T NEED TO SAY ANOTHER WORD, PARDNER. WHAT EVER YOU WANT ME TO DO, IT WON'T BE ENOUGH.

I THINK SONNY COULD SENSE MY ENTHUSIASM... I HADN'T FELT LIKE THIS SINCE THE OLD DAYS WITH LOUIE.

ANDY NEEDS A FRIEND RIGHT NOW AND I DON'T AIM TO DISAPPOINT HIM.

SO WE LEFT RIGHT THEN. WE FILLED UP SONNY'S CAR WITH GAS (HE DIDN'T WANT TO TAKE MY "RICE-BURNER") AND TOOK OFF THAT NIGHT FOR CALIFORNIA.

IN ALL HONESTY, I THINK IT WAS THE BEST TIME I EVER HAD.

38.

IT TOOK THREE WEEKS TO TRACK HER DOWN. SHE HAD A DIFFERENT LAST NAME, BUT SHE STILL LIVED IN LIVERMORE. SONNY HAD SPENT SOME TIME AS A BILL COLLECTOR, SO HE KNEW A FEW TRICKS.

BY THE TIME WE GOT THERE, HE WAS TOTALLY "ON BOARD." IT'S SOMETHING SPECIAL WHEN YOU HAVE A MISSION LIKE THIS AND EVERYTHING STARTS TO FALL INTO PLACE.

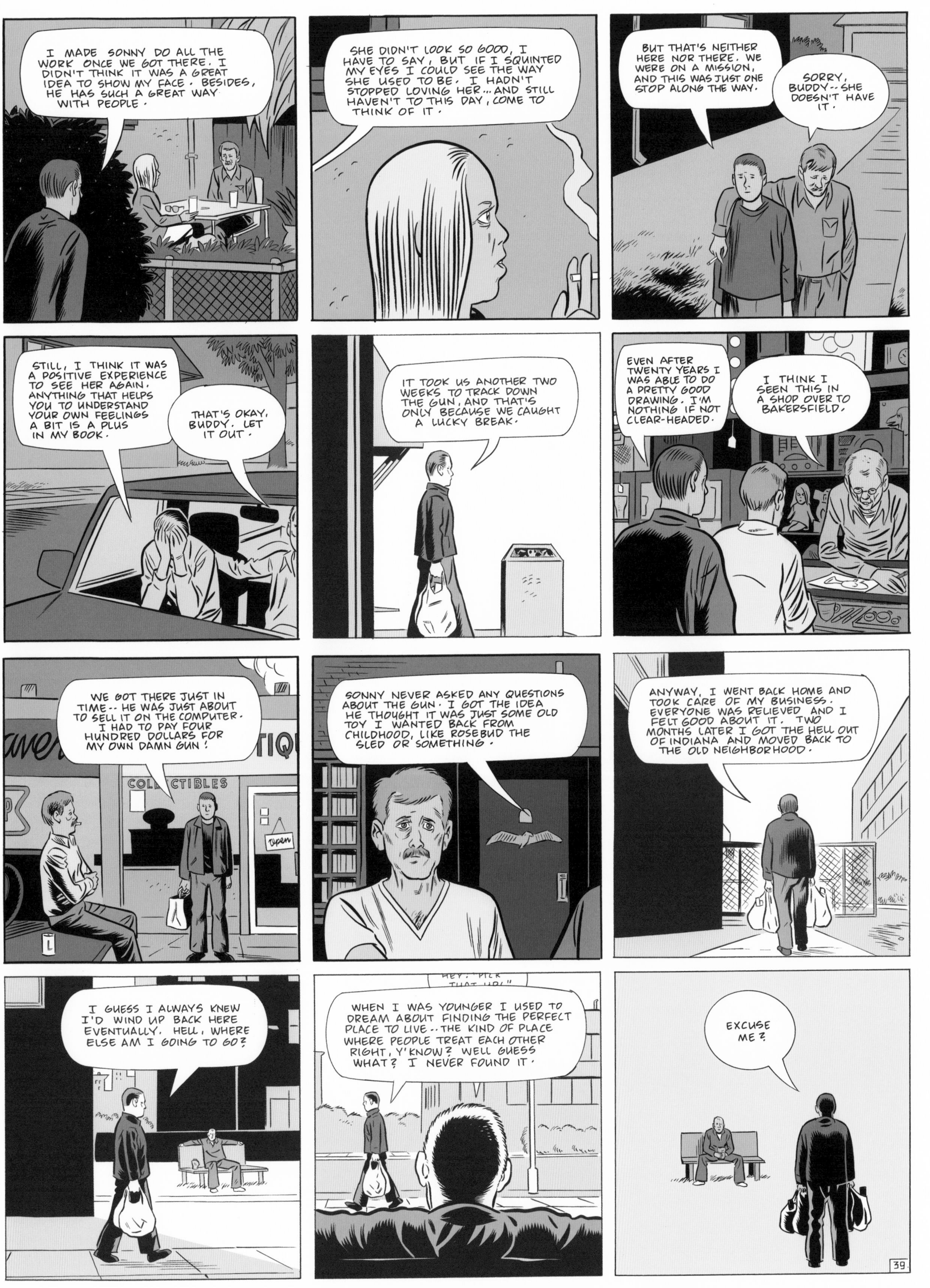
I MADE SONNY DO ALL THE WORK ONCE WE GOT THERE. I DIDN'T THINK IT WAS A GREAT IDEA TO SHOW MY FACE. BESIDES, HE HAS SUCH A GREAT WAY WITH PEOPLE.
SHE DIDN'T LOOK SO GOOD, I HAVE TO SAY, BUT IF I SQUINTED MY EYES I COULD SEE THE WAY SHE USED TO BE. I HADN'T STOPPED LOVING HER... AND STILL HAVEN'T TO THIS DAY, COME TO THINK OF IT.
BUT THAT'S NEITHER HERE NOR THERE. WE WERE ON A MISSION, AND THIS WAS JUST ONE STOP ALONG THE WAY.
SORRY, BUDDY -- SHE DOESN'T HAVE IT.
STILL, I THINK IT WAS A POSITIVE EXPERIENCE TO SEE HER AGAIN. ANYTHING THAT HELPS YOU TO UNDERSTAND YOUR OWN FEELINGS A BIT IS A PLUS IN MY BOOK.
THAT'S OKAY, BUDDY. LET IT OUT.
IT TOOK US ANOTHER TWO WEEKS TO TRACK DOWN THE GUN, AND THAT'S ONLY BECAUSE WE CAUGHT A LUCKY BREAK.
EVEN AFTER TWENTY YEARS I WAS ABLE TO DO A PRETTY GOOD DRAWING. I'M NOTHING IF NOT CLEAR-HEADED.
I THINK I SEEN THIS IN A SHOP OVER TO BAKERSFIELD.
WE GOT THERE JUST IN TIME -- HE WAS JUST ABOUT TO SELL IT ON THE COMPUTER. I HAD TO PAY FOUR HUNDRED DOLLARS FOR MY OWN DAMN GUN!
COLLECTIBLES
Open
SONNY NEVER ASKED ANY QUESTIONS ABOUT THE GUN. I GOT THE IDEA HE THOUGHT IT WAS JUST SOME OLD TOY I WANTED BACK FROM CHILDHOOD, LIKE ROSEBUD THE SLED OR SOMETHING.
ANYWAY, I WENT BACK HOME AND TOOK CARE OF MY BUSINESS. EVERYONE WAS RELIEVED AND I FELT GOOD ABOUT IT. TWO MONTHS LATER I GOT THE HELL OUT OF INDIANA AND MOVED BACK TO THE OLD NEIGHBORHOOD.
I GUESS I ALWAYS KNEW I'D WIND UP BACK HERE EVENTUALLY. HELL, WHERE ELSE AM I GOING TO GO?
WHEN I WAS YOUNGER I USED TO DREAM ABOUT FINDING THE PERFECT PLACE TO LIVE -- THE KIND OF PLACE WHERE PEOPLE TREAT EACH OTHER RIGHT, Y'KNOW? WELL GUESS WHAT? I NEVER FOUND IT.
EXCUSE ME?

THE UNITED STATES OF ANDY

IT'S A DAMN SHAME ABOUT PEOPLE, IT REALLY IS. WE ARE SURELY THE UGLIEST CREATURES IN ALL OF NATURE.

LOOK AT YOU: WHAT HAVE YOU EVER DONE? WHAT GIVES YOU THE CONFIDENCE TO SIT THERE WITH A SMIRK ON YOUR FACE LIKE YOU'RE BETTER THAN ME?

YOU THINK ANYBODY CARES ABOUT YOU? GUESS WHAT--THEY DON'T. YOU CAN LIE TO YOURSELF ALL YOU WANT, BUT THE REST OF US ARE WISE TO YOUR SCAM.

YOU SHOULD HAVE BEEN AN ABORTION OR SOLD INTO SLAVERY. WHO GAVE YOU THE RIGHT TO TAKE UP SPACE IN MY WORLD?

I'VE NEVER DONE ANYTHING TO ANYONE THEY DIDN'T DESERVE. MY JUSTICE IS NOTHING IF NOT MERCIFUL.

DOES THAT MEAN I'M SOFT? HELL NO. YOU THINK I'M AFRAID OF YOU? YOU THINK I'M AFRAID TO ERASE YOU FROM THE LANDSCAPE?

LOOK, I KNOW WHAT YOU'RE THINKING. HELL, MAYBE YOU'RE RIGHT.

IT'S A LOT OF RESPONSIBILITY, BUT I'M NOT ONE TO COMPLAIN. I'VE GOT A JOB TO DO LIKE EVERYONE ELSE.

WHO AM I? YOUR WORST NIGHTMARE.

A COUPLE YEARS AGO I WAS HAULING AWAY SOME JUNK FOR THE LADY UPSTAIRS. HER HUSBAND HAD JUST DIED AND... ANYWAY, I LIKE TO BE OF SERVICE.

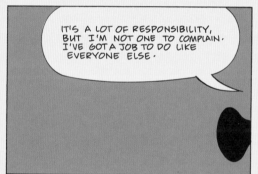

TO MAKE A LONG STORY SHORT, I RAN INTO STOOB AT THE DUMP. FIRST TIME I'D SEEN HIM IN TWENTY YEARS.

TURNS OUT HE RUNS A RECYCLING CENTER ON THE WEST SIDE AND DOES SOMETHING ELSE WITH SOLAR ENERGY OR SOMETHING... A REAL SOLID CITIZEN.

I WONDERED IF HE KNEW HOW LUCKY HE WAS. GUYS LIKE THAT ALWAYS TURN UP ON THEIR FEET. HE EVEN ASKED ABOUT LOUIE, IF YOU CAN BELIEVE IT. MISTER NICE-GUY.

HE COULDN'T FOOL ME. UNDERNEATH IT ALL HE WAS STILL THE SAME GUY.

NOBODY EVER CHANGES.

THAT'S NOT TO SAY THAT EVERYBODY'S AN ASSHOLE. I KNOW BETTER THAN THAT.

HELL, YOU'RE PROBABLY A DECENT PERSON YOURSELF. THERE ARE PLENTY OF YOU OUT THERE.

POP

40.

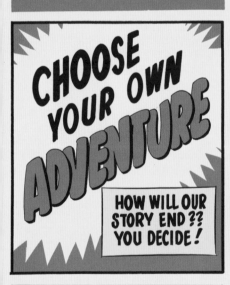

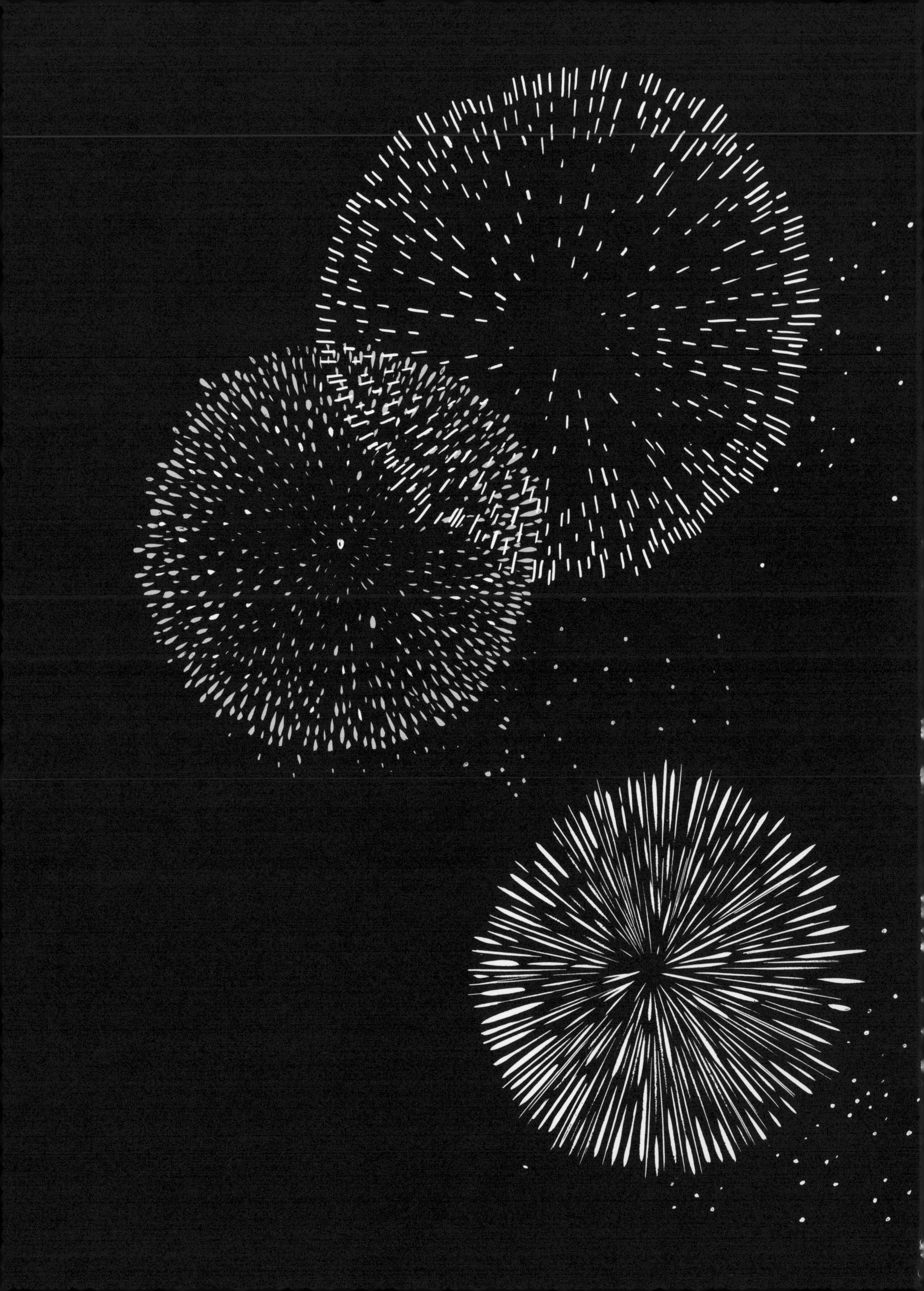

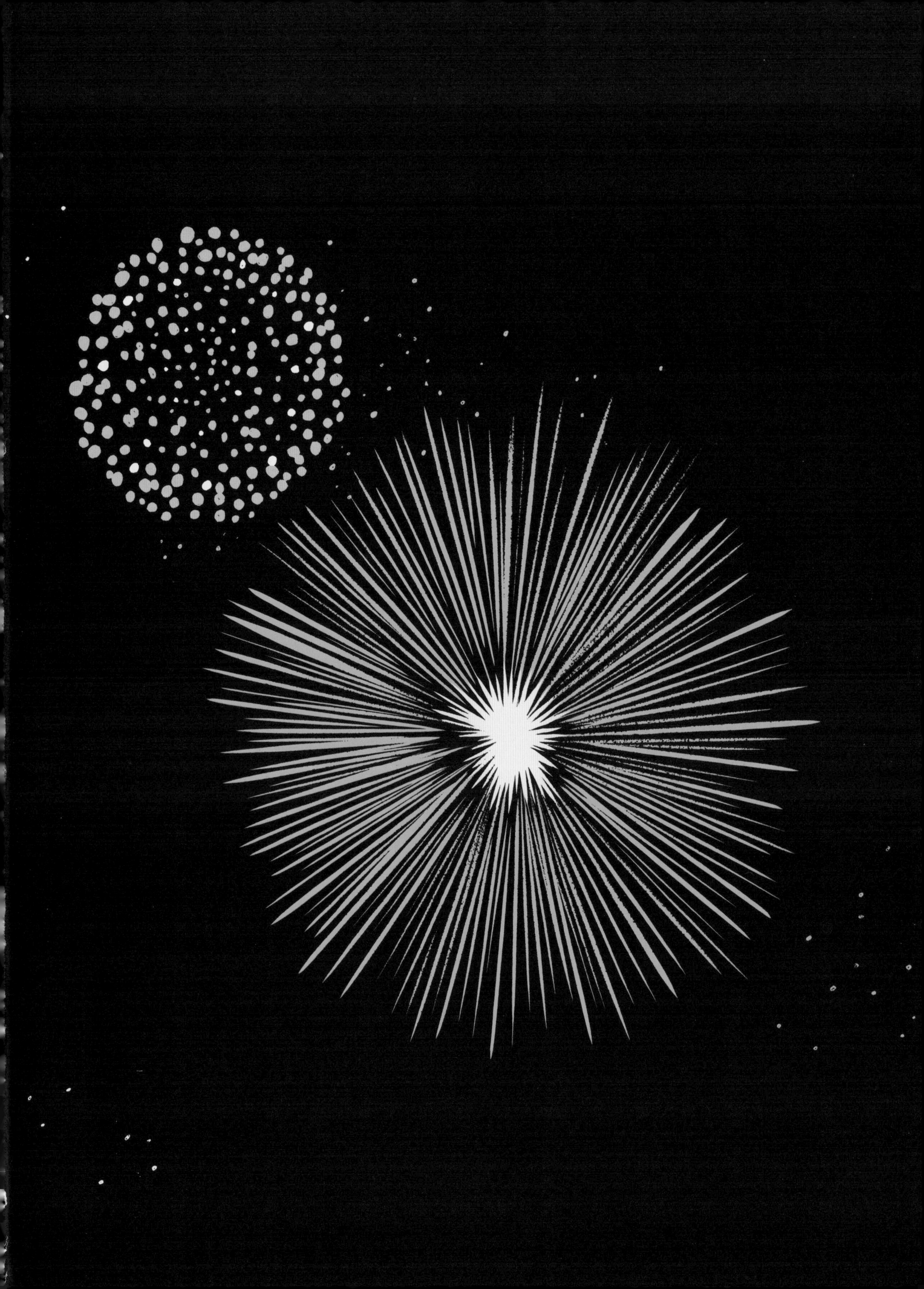

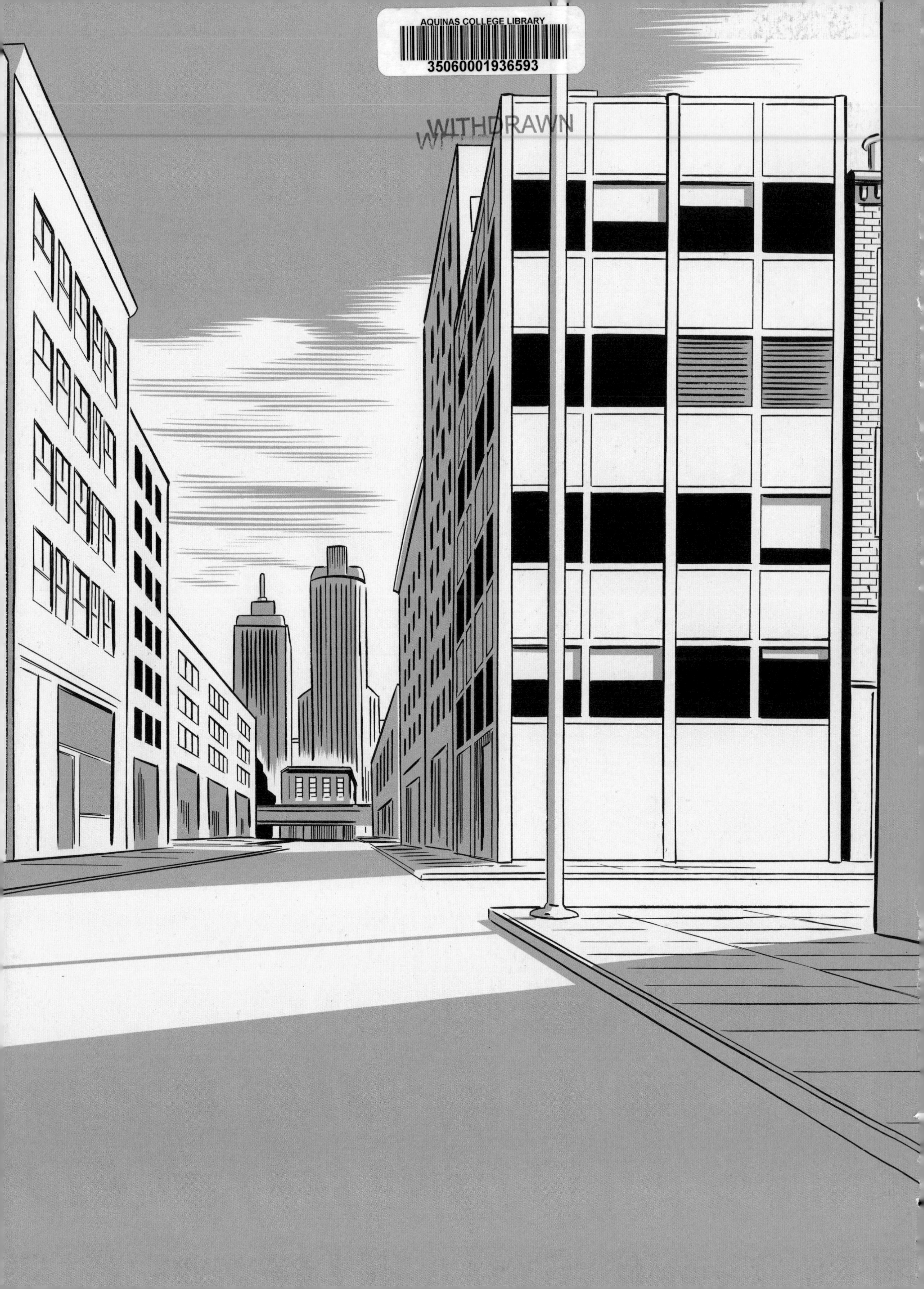